SCHOOLCRAFT COLLEGE LIBRARY

W9-BRQ-276

WITHDRAWN

NEWSWORDY

KEN DACHMAN

Simon and Schuster, Inc.
New York

Copyright © 1985 by Ken Dachman

All rights reserved
including the right of reproduction
in whole or in part in any form

Published by New World Dictionaries/Simon & Schuster
A Division of Simon & Schuster, Inc.
Simon & Schuster Building
Rockefeller Center
1230 Avenue of the Americas
New York, New York 10020

Dictionary Editorial Offices:
New World Dictionaries
850 Euclid Avenue
Cleveland, Ohio 44114

SIMON AND SCHUSTER, TREE OF KNOWLEDGE, WEBSTER'S NEW WORLD
and colophons are trademarks of Simon & Schuster, Inc.

Designed by Publishing Synthesis Ltd./Kenneth R. Ekkens

Manufactured in the United States of America

10 9 8 7 6 5 4 3 2 1

Library of Congress Catalog Card Number: 85-61484

ISBN: 0-671-60067-2

Dedication

I walked into Dave and Pat Turner's lives seven years ago. They did everything possible to make me feel welcome and loved; and they succeeded.

Now it's my turn. I dedicate this work to you, Mom and Pop, with all my love and respect.

Acknowledgements

Two of Simon & Schuster's finest, Felecia Abbadessa and Meg Medina, encouraged me from the very start. Felecia's meticulous editing saved me from a number of embarrassments.

I could never have survived this past year without the friendship of Peter Warner, attorney extraordinaire. His jokes (frequently awful) and unwavering support guided me through some difficult times.

Ken Bernstein, my "pen pal," spent hours listening to me babble on about issues and ideas, most of which, I'm sure, made no sense at all.

Finally, a special thanks goes to John Whalen, whose editorial and research talent is evidenced throughout this work.

Introduction

What's news? Anything and everything, it would seem, depending on whom one asks.

Keeping abreast of current events is, surely, no small task. News issues are about as volatile as campaign promises, as voluminous as the federal deficit.

It's no great surprise, then, that many folks have given up on the news, preferring a surrender to ignorance over the endless tangle of facts and figures packaged for the local "dailies" and performed in living rooms across America.

The blame for this burgeoning news apathy should not rest entirely with the mass-media, however. News, after all, is a business subject to requisite time and space limitations.

Still, those very limitations inevitably weaken the bridge between news proliferation and news dissemination—the bridge that *NewsWordy*, I trust, will effectively mend while guiding you comfortably (at your own pace) through the often intolerable, always exciting, maze of today's headline matter.

What's *NewsWordy?* A collection of news-words—the terms, phrases, labels, titles, and journalistic jargon essential to understanding current events. Reading *NewsWordy* will afford you a general grasp of most, if not all, areas of the news. Equal consideration is given to economic, political, national, and international newswords. And though I've probably left out an important word or two, I feel quite certain you'll enjoy the scope and diversity of the entries.

So read cover to cover or browse if you like. But don't ever give up on the news. Life's most lasting satisfaction, you'll find, comes from a fundamental understanding of the world in which we live.

Acid Rain

is the term used to describe rain, snow, or other precipitation that has been contaminated by a variety of acids.

Concentrations of sulfuric and nitric acids are formed in the atmosphere when water vapor in the air mixes with chemical wastes released from cars, trucks, trains, factories, and power plants that burn coal or oil.

Acid rain falls over large areas of North America and Europe, polluting thousands of lakes, rivers, and streams, killing fish and other aquatic life. The toxic precipitation is most prevalent east of the Mississippi River and has its greatest impact in the Adirondack Mountains of New York, and in eastern and central Canada.

There is evidence that acid rain accelerates the erosion of older statues and buildings. Historical landmarks and works of art made of stone or bronze are being moved indoors to protect them from premature deterioration.

Acid rain is the source of considerable friction between the United States and Canada, where large numbers of lakes are dying as the result of pollutants released from factories in the United States.

Canada has strongly protested U.S. "inaction" in controlling sulphur-dioxide emissions, and U.S. refusals to accept the cause and effect relationship between emissions and acid rain. In response to those protests, President Reagan's 1984 State of the Union address included a plea to Congress to double funding for acid-rain research.

In November of 1984, the Environmental Protection Agency (EPA) proposed new regulations for industrial smokestacks, which would require the installation of scrubbers to remove sulphur residues from smoke, or, as an alternative, the use of low-sulphur coal.

Ironically, previous EPA legislation—the Clean Air Act of 1970—may have exacerbated the acid rain problem. Rather than cleaning up emissions to meet pollution standards imposed by that law, many industries simply built taller smokestacks, ensuring that smoke particles would be lifted into the upper atmosphere, instead of falling in a factory's immediate vicinity where they would be detected.

Unforeseen in 1970 was the possibility that upper air currents would carry sulfurous emissions hundreds of miles, where they would fall in the form of acid rain into ecologically sensitive territory.

The costs of eliminating the sources of acid rain are substantial—an estimated initial outlay of from $1 to 5 billion and annual recurring costs from $300 million to $1.4 billion. Decreasing acid rain's effects through the addition of lime or other neutralizing agents to damaged lakes also carries a staggering price tag.

Acquired Immune Deficiency Syndrome (AIDS)

first appeared in the United States in 1981. The disease destroys the body's immune system, leaving the AIDS victim virtually defenseless against a host of infections.

By the end of 1984, AIDS had stricken more than seventy-seven hundred in the United States, resulting in over thirty-three hundred deaths. High-risk groups for AIDS are clustered in urban areas, particularly in New York, San Francisco, and Los Angeles, and include active homosexual and bisexual men (71 percent), intravenous drug users—especially heroin users (17 percent), and Haitian immigrants (5 percent). Other high-risk groups include hemophiliacs and partners of bisexual men. Men are at higher risk than women; over 90 percent of AIDS victims are males between the ages of twenty and forty-nine. In the United States 7 percent of AIDS victims are female.

Researchers have advanced two theories about the causes of AIDS. One is that the immune system of the victim is simply overpowered by the assault of a variety of infections to which members of the high-risk groups are constantly exposed. The other is that AIDS is caused by a specific virus.

In the spring of 1984, a team of researchers at Harvard Medical School's National Cancer Institute isolated and mapped the genetic material of a virus believed to cause AIDS. At about the same time, French researchers announced that they had discovered an almost identical AIDS virus. These findings are expected to advance dramatically the chances of detection, prevention, and treatment of the deadly disease.

Five companies are attempting to develop tests to detect the virus in the blood. The Food and Drug Administration recently approved clinical trials of an AIDS vaccine called Interleukin-2, a genetically engineered form of a natural protein that enhances the effectiveness of the body's immune system.

Adjustable-Rate Mortgages (ARMs)

are housing loans with interest rates that fluctuate annually in accord with market levels.

During 1984, ARMs accounted for over 60 percent of new mortgages and were credited with helping to sustain the strongest U.S. housing boom since 1975. One study reported that more than five million Americans who could not qualify for standard (fixed-rate) mortgages were able to buy homes using the ARM approach.

The initial monthly cost of an ARM loan is generally low, reflecting a discount from prevailing interest rates. At the end of each year, the loan's interest rate is adjusted upward, ending the discount and bringing the rate up to standard levels. From that point on, the loan's interest rate can go up or down, depending on the market. ARMs sometimes include a cap, which limits interest-rate increases.

Even so, the monthly costs of some ARM loans can rise sharply, which leads, some critics claim, to delinquencies and foreclosures.

Most homebuyers using ARM loans plan for their incomes to increase along with their monthly payments. The trouble is that many homebuyers don't realize what relatively small increases in interest rates can do to their monthly payments. A 9 percent loan on a $56,000 mortgage, for example, requires a monthly payment of about $450. When the interest rate rises to 10 percent, the monthly cost of the loan becomes $620. Should inflation (see Inflation) or another factor in the credit market cause the ARM rate to go to 15 percent, the monthly payment rises to $707.

Buyers who take out ARM loans are being advised to shop carefully and to be realistic in projecting the potential expenses the loan could generate in the future.

Affirmative Action

policies, introduced during the early 1960s and enforced with varying degrees of zeal since, are U.S. government guidelines designed to encourage firmly the employment of minorities and women.

The government promotes affirmative action on the grounds that some action needs to be taken in order to make up for two hundred years of discrimination against minority groups.

Specific affirmative action policies include offering remedial or compensatory training, aggressive recruiting of minorities and women, and revising employment tests and applications to delete discriminatory elements.

Afghanistan,

a Central Asian country about the size of Texas, has been a bloody battleground since December 1979, when an estimated forty thousand Soviet troops invaded its borders.

The Soviets claimed that the "assistance" was necessary to aid the Marxist regime of Hafizullah Amin in stifling a Moslem rebellion. But Amin was killed shortly before the invasion, and evidence suggests that Soviet "advisers" had carried out the assassination. Amin's successor, Babrak Karmal welcomed the Russian "stabilization" of his new government.

Many observers saw the invasion as a logical extension of the Soviet Union's historic impulse to install friendly regimes —either by force or subversion—in the countries on which it borders. Others suggested that geography prompted the action. Its presence in Afghanistan positions the USSR closer to the oil fields and warm-water ports of the Middle East.

Afghanistan, an independent nation since 1919, was formerly part of the British Empire. The country was ruled by a king until 1963, which was the beginning of a decade of constitutional monarchy. A Marxist group seized power in 1978, encountering fierce Moslem resistance which continues today, despite the presence of over 100,000 Soviet troops and a staggering array of military hardware.

Afghan guerrillas, many fighting with weapons fifty to one hundred years old, have kept the Soviets at bay for more than five years, but it appears that the Soviet Union is winning the war. Although the rebels control the country's high, bleak mountains and treacherous valleys, the Soviets dominate the cities, where most of Afghanistan's fifteen million people live.

Over 500,000 Afghans have been killed or wounded since 1979; four million have fled to other countries. Tens of thousands of children have been taken from their parents and sent to the Soviet Union for "education."

International organizations monitoring Soviet conduct in Afghanistan have reported "crimes of indiscriminate warfare combined with the worst excesses of unbridled violence against civilians." Refugees have charged the Soviets with burning civilians alive, grenading women and children, dynamiting elderly farmers, and using chemical warfare. Rebels (and suspected rebels) have been forced to lie down on roads to be crushed by Soviet tanks.

On the fifth anniversary of the Soviet invasion, critics of arms control talks between the United States and the USSR cited Soviet "butchery" in Afghanistan as evidence that these discussions are futile. The Soviet Union, these critics argue, is violating the Geneva Convention and other human rights agreements in Afghanistan.

Agent Orange

is the military's code name for a dioxin-laced herbicide used extensively in Vietnam to defoliate forests. Thousands of Vietnam veterans blame exposure to Agent Orange for cancers and birth defects.

A long legal battle ended in 1985 when a federal judge arranged a $180 million settlement from seven chemical companies. Even after settlement was reached, a major problem remained: distributing the funds fairly to the 170,000 veterans and families who had filed claims. The court planned to hold public hearings beginning in March 1985, but the settlement pool was seen by most observers as clearly inadequate. Federal assistance to Agent Orange victims was called for by several principals in the case. "Unless Congress provides comprehensive help," said one attorney, "anything the court succeeds in doing will be a Band-Aid."

There was a side note to the Agent Orange settlement. Attorneys who had worked on the case requested $23.5 million in fees. The court cut legal fees to $9.3 million—to be paid from interest earned by the settlement pool.

Alzheimer's Disease

is a devastating brain disorder which wipes out memory and deadens the mind.

Named after the German neurologist who first described it, Alzheimer's disease strikes men and women, usually without warning and for no apparent reason. While most victims are in their 50s and 60s, it frequently appears in people still in their 40s, and, on rare occasions, even younger.

Alzheimer's develops gradually, over four to ten years. Symptoms include memory loss, impaired judgment, disorientation, and the loss of language skills. Personality changes are also common. As mental abilities slowly decline, physical problems, such as difficulty in walking, emerge.

The cause of Alzheimer's disease is unknown, but there are two theories about its source. Some scientists believe that the disorder may grow out of the brain's response to injury. Others think it is caused by some specific agent—a virus, a toxin, a genetic trait, or some environmental substance.

Because there is no cure for the disorder, clinics for Alzheimer's concentrate on treating the patient's family. "Our goal is to keep families together and the patient at home," said Sue Deinard of a University of Minnesota clinic.

Common sense, stress reduction, and lots of patience are the keys to managing the disease, according to Deinard. Families are advised to provide a carefully structured environment for the Alzheimer's patient, many of whom can function quite well with family support.

Amnesty International,

a worldwide human rights organization, is devoted to helping people imprisoned for political or religious beliefs—provided that these dissidents have not used or advocated violence.

Since its founding in 1961, Amnesty International has secured the release of tens of thousands of political prisoners. Based in London, Amnesty International has offices in thirty-five countries. In 1977, the organization won a Nobel Peace Prize for "advancing the cause of freedom, justice, and, thereby, peace in the world."

Amnesty International issues human rights reports, monitors prison conditions, and protests political oppression. Its activities in recent months have included: an accusation that at least two hundred Soviet citizens are confined to mental institutions because of their political beliefs; an investigation into the high number of deaths occurring in Turkish military prisons; an exposé of torture in Quebec jails; criticism of Northern Ireland court proceedings in which Catholics were convicted of crimes and imprisoned without jury trials based only on the uncontested word of informants; and a protest of the "barbaric torture" of Iranian dissidents by the Khomeini government.

Andrology

is a new medical specialty devoted to the treatment of infertility in men.

As recently as 1960, doctors believed that 90 percent of barren marriages were caused by women's medical problems. Today, experts agree that male reproductive disorders account for a couple's inability to have children about half the time.

"The field is still quite new," said Dr. Ira Sharlip, an andrologist at the University of California Medical Center. "Our knowledge about male infertility is incomplete."

Causes of male infertility identified to date include abnormalities in the veins, bacterial infections, drugs, smoking, alcohol, exposure to extreme heat, fever, hot tubs, and underwear that is too tight. Pesticides, industrial chemicals, X-rays, radioactive substances, and prolonged stress can also cause reproductive problems.

Although male infertility usually can be treated once detected, the attention of most fertility experts remains directed toward women.

Dr. Mary Ann Bartusis, a psychiatry professor at the Medical College of Pennsylvania, said that infertile men often refuse to accept the truth. "They'll say 'It can't be me.' They'll keep telling their wives to be patient and they are very reluctant to be tested."

Bartusis indicated that men refuse to acknowledge the possibility of infertility for a variety of reasons: the shame which accompanies not being a "real" man, ambivalent feelings about fatherhood, uncertainty about their marriages, and, most commonly, the fear that their wives will leave them for a man with whom they can have children. (Studies of childless marriages indicate that only a small percentage break up because of infertility.)

Angola

extends for about one thousand miles along the Atlantic coast of Africa. Once a Portuguese colony, Angola gained its independence in 1975 and is now ruled by a Marxist "people's republic," although large areas of the country are controlled by a rebel group called the National Union for the Total Independence of Angola (UNITA).

The Angolan government relies on extensive military support from Cuba and the Soviet Union to stay in power. The United States supplied covert aid to Angolan rebels until 1976 when Congress terminated the program.

Since taking office, President Reagan has frequently cited Angola as an example of Soviet "world domination" techniques. When a group of Zairean refugees invaded neighboring Zaire from Angola, the Reagan administration charged that the invasion had been engineered by Cuban and Soviet advisers in Angola. Reagan asked Congress to renew aid to the UNITA group on several occasions but has been turned down repeatedly.

The Reagan administration has refused to grant Angola diplomatic recognition until Cuban troops leave, despite requests of the U.S. companies (such as Gulf Oil) operating in Angola.

Annuity

is an insurance vehicle through which a lump sum investment is returned, significantly larger, years later.

Income earned during the life of an annuity is tax deferred, and returns are usually high (only slightly less than those paid by the best bonds). Upon maturity, there are several options for pay out: lump sum, over a fixed number of years, or for the duration of a person's life.

With an increasing public awareness that whole life insurance is often a terrible investment, more and more insurance companies are offering annuities. Owners of professional sports teams are also finding annuities useful in paying for the seven-figure salaries often demanded by top players. When a star halfback is reported to have signed a $9.6 million contract, it is likely that the total will be paid twenty years from now, out of the proceeds of an annuity purchased for considerably less.

Anorexia Nervosa

is a psychosomatic eating disorder most common among teenage girls. For reasons not known, the disease has become more prevalent in recent years (perhaps because of America's growing preoccupation with fitness and vanity) and now afflicts about 1 percent of young American women, and a small number of men. When undetected or untreated, anorexia nervosa results in death through self-starvation.

Some psychologists have theorized that anorexia nervosa is prompted by: leaving home for the first time, intense competition at school, severe depression, pressure from family and friends to lose weight, sexual fear, confusion, drug usage, and discontinuation of the use of birth control pills.

In anorexia nervosa's early stages, the anorectic simply goes on a strict diet. As the disorder progresses, however, most anorectics stop eating altogether. Although most anorectics are only slightly overweight when they stop eating, all believe they are extremely fat, a belief they cling to adamantly even as they become emaciated.

Soon after her fast begins, the anorectic's menstrual periods cease. She sleeps poorly but remains physically active, even hyperactive in some cases. Eventually, the anorectic's body temperature declines to dangerously low levels. Food becomes repulsive and the anorectic is physically unable to eat even if she wanted to.

Emergency treatment of the disorder usually involves hospitalization and intravenous "force feeding." Long-term treatment requires behavioral counseling.

About half of the women afflicted with anorexia nervosa recover permanently; 10 percent die of self-imposed starvation. For the rest, temporary recovery alternates with frequent relapse.

Antitrust Laws

are intended to allay unfair competition and restraint of trade. Business practices outlawed by antitrust legislation include monopolies, corporations with exclusive control of a product or service; trusts, a combination of companies controlled by a single board of trustees; and cartels, similar to trusts but without a formal governing board.

In 1985, U.S. Commerce Secretary Malcolm Baldrige proposed repeal of some antitrust restrictions to allow mergers so that U.S. firms could deal more effectively with foreign competition. Supporters of Baldrige's proposal contend that it would remove roadblocks which prohibit American companies from becoming involved in joint ventures similar to those routinely undertaken by German and Japanese firms.

Apartheid,

which means "apartness," is the name given to the nation of South Africa's rigid system of racial segregation. The apartheid policy, called "separate development" by the South African government, is designed to maintain the economic and political supremacy of the country's white minority.

There are four groups that apartheid keeps strictly separated: blacks (67 percent of the population); whites (of European descent—19 percent); coloreds (of mixed black, white, Asian descent—11 percent); and Asians (mostly from India—about 3.7 percent).

The white minority controls all aspects of South African life. Separate housing and education laws are strictly enforced. Intermarriage is prohibited, and even associations between racial groups are frowned upon. The white government has set aside ten areas within the country for use as black "homelands," but these areas have few economic resources. The government has forcibly relocated an estimated three-and-a-half-million people since 1960.

The majority of South African blacks work in white areas, but must live in tightly segregated districts. All blacks must carry passes and use segregated public facilities. Only whites may vote in elections, serve in parliament, work for the government in responsible positions. South Africa's twenty-one million blacks have no representation at all.

The United Nations and about every country in the world have criticized apartheid as a glaring violation of human rights.

South African products have been boycotted in many nations, and South African citizens were excluded from the Olympic Games and other international events.

In the United States, apartheid has been the target of frequent protests by students and civil rights groups. Congressional leaders (such as Senator Kennedy of Massachusetts) have spoken forcefully in condemnation of this segregationist policy.

The white South African government defends apartheid, claiming that white rule has made South Africa the richest and most stable nation on the African continent. White leaders also claim that "many" South African nonwhites favor apartheid, because blacks in South Africa earn more and live better than blacks in other African countries.

Late in 1984, major disturbances in black areas prompted the South African government to offer "an informal forum" in which the grievances of blacks could be heard. When anti-apartheid leaders (including Nobel Peace Prize winner and Anglican bishop, Desmond Tutu) rejected this offer, the government quickly reverted to a confrontational approach. In February 1985, South African police, attempting to quell a riot outside Capetown, killed eighteen people, and injured two hundred others.

The governments of the United States and Western European nations seem to tolerate apartheid, perhaps because South Africa is considered to be strongly anti-communist, or because its healthy economy offers profitable opportunities for investors in valuable minerals and strategic raw materials.

American blacks and human rights activists have strongly protested the Reagan administration's South African policies. The Carter administration, U.S. black leaders have pointed out, was instrumental in ending apartheid in the African nation of Zimbabwe (formerly Rhodesia).

Arbitration

is the process by which the parties to a dispute defer to the judgment of a neutral third party.

With an epidemic of litigation choking the nation's judicial system, court-administered arbitration systems have been established by more than one hundred trial courts across the country.

A study done in the Pittsburgh court system by the Rand Corporation's Institute for Civil Justice reported that the average time for cases to reach resolution was reduced from two years to seventy days through use of the arbitration process. Total costs per case were cut by over 90 percent.

Generally, arbitration is limited to civil suits valued from $10,000 to $20,000. Opposing parties submit their dispute to review by a neutral arbitrator, who considers both positions and decides the case. Depending upon the ground rules agreed to beforehand, arbitration decisions may be binding or open to appeal.

In 1984, a group of nationwide insurance companies established a pilot arbitration program. Under this program—the Arbitration Forum—the insurance companies agree to compulsory arbitration of property damage disputes of less than $25,000 arising from auto accidents. The program guarantees disposition of all disputes within fifty-one days. Policyholders, meanwhile, collect without delay under collision provisions of their policies.

"If we could resolve more cases through arbitration, we could reduce our attorneys' fees dramatically," said Al Kenyon, vice president of claims for Kemper Insurance. "Ultimately, we can pass these savings on to the consumer."

Arbitration has long been a staple in labor disputes and is used frequently in major-league baseball to settle player contracts.

Many retired judges, including Joseph Wopner of television's *People's Court*, are willing to act as arbitrators.

Argentina,

though blessed with abundant farmland and rich in natural resources, has been struggling to keep itself together for thirty years.

The second-largest country in South America (after Brazil), Argentina is about a third the size of the United States. After gaining its independence from Spain in 1816, Argentina created a thriving cattle industry, and, later, an extensive system of railroads, mining, and manufacturing enterprises.

Unfortunately, economic promise never brought political stability, and between 1920 and 1966 Argentina was the site of seven military coups. In 1943, Colonel Juan Peron became the minister of labor. He strengthened Argentina's unions and gave workers higher wages, more holidays, and increased benefits. With the support of urban workers (previously ignored by the government), Peron was elected president in 1946 and named his second wife, Eva, as his chief assistant.

Under the Perons, government spending increased greatly. Manufacturing wages, worker welfare programs, and Eva Peron's Social Aid Foundation grants were paid for by higher and higher taxes. To curb protests of his policies, Peron suppressed freedom of speech, and dealt harshly with the courts, the media, universities, and Argentina's politically powerful Catholic church.

In 1955, army and navy officers deposed Peron who fled to Spain. Peron's government had left Argentina nearly bankrupt. Large debts, runaway inflation, and low productivity continued, resulting in strikes and violence wherever an attempt was made to enforce austerity measures.

In 1973, Peron returned to Argentina's presidency. When he died in 1974, his third wife, Isabel, became Argentina's leader and the first woman president in the Western Hemisphere.

Military governments came and went until 1981 when General Leopoldo Galtieri took power. Galtieri's forces invaded the Falkland Islands in 1982, proclaiming them for Argentina (under their original Spanish name, Malvinas). Great Britain responded with an armada and five thousand marines. Argentina surrendered in June 1982 and Galtieri resigned.

Democracy returned to Argentina in 1983, with the re vival of a constitution providing for a federal union of the country's twenty-two provinces. New president Raúl Alfonsín, elected in 1983, finds his nation trying to cope with a 60 percent inflation rate (*see* Inflation) and $45 billion in foreign debt. Argentina is the world's third-largest debtor and fears of default have plagued foreign banks (including some in the United States) for several years. Alfonsín's administration has agreed to austerity (*see* Austerity) measures and pledged to repay Argentina's debt.

Artificial Ear,

an electronic device that can be attached to the auditory nerve, has the potential to restore hearing to several million profoundly deaf people and, possibly, to tens of millions afflicted with severe hearing impairments.

The device costs about $10,000; the operation about $7,000. In a four-hour procedure, surgeons attach seven electrodes to the patient's auditory nerve and create an artificial opening in which the wires terminate just behind the ear. After a one-week healing period the wires are connected to a microprocessor the size of a cigarette package. The processor, which contains a microphone, sends signals to the auditory nerve.

According to Dr. Joseph B. Nudol, a surgeon at the Massachusetts Eye and Ear Infirmary, a patient with the artificial ear "will be able to distinguish about 70 percent of words spoken to him." The seven-electrode artificial ear is considered a dramatic improvement over the long-used single-electrode device which allows the deaf person to hear noise, but not human speech. It is even further removed from the ordinary hearing aid, which is not directly connected to the auditory nerve, but instead uses only a tiny microphone, amplifier, and speaker.

Artificial Intelligence (AI)

is a branch of computer science attempting to "teach" computers to think like humans. AI efforts have not been very successful, except to highlight how little science knows about the workings of the human thought process.

Computers can mimic human thinking in highly structured situations. The machines are ultralogical; they follow rules well, and calculate accurately and quickly. But computer software lacks the perception, intuition, understanding, and flexibility of the human thought process. Human intelligence,

AI experts have learned, includes not only the application of learned rules, but mental skills and common sense problem-solving abilities which, to date, cannot be programmed.

Even in the structured world of chess, computers have not learned to "learn." Despite playing the game since the late 1950s, no computer has beaten a human chess champion.

Aspartame

is rapidly replacing saccharin as the nation's favorite synthetic sweetener. Manufactured by G. D. Searle of Chicago, Illinois, aspartame is marketed under the name NutraSweet. (Searle also markets an aspartame-based sugar substitute called Equal.)

Dozens of food and beverage manufacturers have been licensed to use aspartame in their products. NutraSweet can be found in gelatin desserts, milkshake powders, instant coffee, and puddings. Unfortunately, aspartame breaks down under extreme heat and so is not very useful in cooking. Searle says that it is working toward remedying this shortcoming.

Recently, most U.S. soft-drink companies have begun using NutraSweet in their diet products. When aspartame first became available, however, it was so expensive that diet drinks were sweetened with a blend of saccharin and NutraSweet. By using NutraSweet exclusively, the soft-drink manufacturers can eliminate saccharin's well-known and largely detested aftertaste.

In addition to its sugarlike taste, aspartame has other attractive qualities. The sweetener is made from protein components which appear naturally in many foods, and is sodium-free. Unlike saccharin, aspartame has never been linked with any general health problems although sufferers of a rare blood disorder (phenyketonuria) are advised not to use it. The substance can also be dangerous to insomniacs and those afflicted with Parkinson's disease.

Austerity

has come to mean a severe reduction in government spending and borrowing—a national "belt tightening"—usually followed by a general decline in that country's standard of living.

Baby Fae

lived for three weeks with the heart of a baboon. Her short life raised a host of medical and ethical issues.

Born in October 1984, in Barstow, California, Baby Fae was afflicted with a fatal congenital deformity which rendered the left side of her heart useless. Shortly after her condition was diagnosed, Baby Fae was brought to Loma Linda University Medical Center sixty miles east of Los Angeles.

Dr. Leonard Bailey, chief of Pediatric Heart Surgery at Loma Linda, proposed that the heart of a young baboon be transplanted into Baby Fae. Baboons, Bailey reasoned, might be better sources of new organs for babies than humans, since healthy infant hearts are rarely available because defective hearts are a leading cause of infant death.

Bailey had (for seven years) transplanted organs between species of newborn animals and was encouraged by the results.

Baby Fae's mother agreed to the operation, and, after considerable deliberation, so did the hospital's board, apparently willing to risk the world's reaction to a somewhat bizarre procedure, in deference to Bailey's character and experience.

In preparing for the operation, the surgical team discovered that a baboon's heart could be more compatible with a patient's tissue than some human hearts. The baboon chosen was a year-old, seven-pound female.

The transplant occurred October 26, 1984, in a four-hour operation. Reaction was mixed: astonishment, curiosity, and approval on one hand; outrage and doubt on the other.

The operation was a "xenograft" (a cross-species transplant). Despite the fact that pig valves are often used in heart surgery and pig skin in burn treatment, animal rights advocates picketed the hospital with signs calling the transplant "Ghoulish Tinkering at Fae's Expense."

Dr. Bailey took up an almost constant vigil in Baby Fae's room. For a time the infant thrived, capturing the hearts of millions via television. But on November 15th, Baby Fae died, a victim of kidney failure (a common complication of major surgery).

Medical experts reviewing the case concluded that the xenograft process needs further study before being attempted again, and suggested that the procedure be used only as a stopgap measure, to keep a fatally ill infant alive until a human donor can be found.

Backpack Nukes

is the name given by U.S. commandos to lightweight nuclear bombs designed for use behind enemy lines in the event of a European war with the Soviet Union.

Technically, the backpack nukes are portable warheads weighing about fifty-eight pounds each, and are formally known as Special Atomic Demolition Munitions.

The small bombs were first produced in 1963 and now, according to NBC News, about a hundred of them are located in West Germany, where special-operations teams are being trained to operate them. According to NBC's sources, "the backpack nukes would be set off by remote control after placement, to destroy targets such as Soviet airfields and command sites." While the Pentagon has confirmed that the portable bombs exist, it has refused to comment on their deployment or use.

Back Pain,

according to Dr. Augustus White of Harvard Medical School, is "the most common and most serious non-life-threatening health problem in the United States."

White, author of *Your Aching Back,* estimates that 60 to 80 percent of adults have significant back pain at some point in their lives.

The expense associated with back disorders (time lost from work and medical bills) has reached $12 to $14 billion a year. A penny from each 22¢ stamp, for example, goes to pay for the backaches experienced by postal employees.

Bagman

is the pickup-and-delivery specialist who acts as the middleman in a variety of illegal transactions. Depending on the kind of illicit exchange taking place, the bagman can be a congressional aide, an alderman's flunkie, a cop, or a bookie's collector.

Ballistic Missiles

are sophisticated, self-propelled weapons consisting of a rocket and one or more warheads (explosive devices). These missiles are unguided during flight. Where they come down is determined by the angle at which they are fired and amount of thrust (power) used in their launching.

About midway through its flight into the atmosphere, a ballistic missile's rocket engine burns out. The trajectory of its descent from that point is determined by gravity, assisted slightly by steering devices in the missile's nose cone or small thruster motors controlled by electronic guidance systems.

After the rocket burns out, most of the ballistic missile drops away, leaving the "payload" (the warhead) to continue on to the target. Missile technology has reached the point where warheads can reach remote targets thousands of miles away with an amazingly high degree of accuracy.

There are several categories of ballistic missiles, including: ICBM (Intercontinental), SLBM (Submarine-Launched), and IRBM (Intermediate-Range).

Bankruptcy

The United States Bankruptcy Code, specifically the Chapter 11 section (also known as Reorganization), allows a creditors' committee and a federal court to supervise a faltering company's operations until profitability—or at least solvency—can be reestablished. If that proves impossible, the bankruptcy court presides over liquidation of the company's assets.

Prior to 1978, bankruptcy was possible only if a company's liabilities exceeded its assets. Since 1978, bankruptcy has been permitted if severe financial difficulties can be "foreseen."

In late 1983, Continental Airlines filed for bankruptcy under the "impending difficulty" provision, suspended its operations, and, under the protection of the bankruptcy court, quickly revived its service with one-third of its former work force at one-half their former wages.

Unions representing Continental's pilots, flight attendants, and mechanics filed suit, charging that the airline had gone into bankruptcy to break union contracts.

Similar charges had been leveled previously against Bildisco, a New Jersey trucking company. When the Bildisco case reached the Supreme Court in February 1984, the court ruled (in a five to four vote) that a bankruptcy court could, indeed, dissolve labor contracts—if these contracts could be proven "burdensome" and a real obstacle to reorganization. The company and the bankruptcy court, the ruling indicated, had an obligation to creditors and shareholders to attempt to continue doing business. The decision applied to the Continental case.

Union officials reacted angrily. William Winpisinger, president of the machinists' union, called the decision "outrageous." Laurence Gold, special counsel to the AFL-CIO, said that the ruling "obviously enhances the opportunity for union busting techniques."

John Jerome, a New York bankruptcy lawyer, disagreed. "I don't think any company in its right mind is going to file for bankruptcy unless it's in real financial trouble," Jerome said. "Sure, you might threaten the unions, but you're not going to file just because you think your wages are too high. Bankruptcy is supposed to be used as a shield, not as a sword."

Barbara Boxer,

a Democratic congresswoman from California, has become an outspoken leader in the movement to curb runaway defense spending.

Boxer wears a metal ring on a chain around her neck. She says that the ring, a fighter plane spare part, is worth $20 but cost the Pentagon $850.

In 1984, Boxer made headlines by publicizing $74,000 ladders and $7,600 coffee pots. Despite the fact that her district includes several defense plants, Boxer was re-elected with 68 percent of the vote.

Battered Wives

are victims of what one police official calls "the quiet criminal plague of American life." An estimated 5.7 million U.S. women are assaulted by their husbands or the men they live with each year. "Even in a nation with a high rate of street violence, women are at a greater risk in their own homes," said a New Hampshire sociologist.

Recently, battered wives in Washington, Oregon, and Minnesota have gained a measure of protection under new laws requiring the immediate—automatic—arrest whenever police find evidence of domestic assault. Penalties for "wife abuse" usually include two days of jail and compulsory counseling.

Although police response to domestic assault traditionally has been the "walk around the block and cool off" approach, an increasing number of law enforcement authorities contend that mandatory arrest laws would have some significant value in breaking the domestic brutality cycle. Studies have shown, for example, that a battered wife's exposure to subsequent assaults is two-and-a-half times greater when the first incidence of violence does not result in arrest.

Too frequently, feminists (see Feminist) contend, police arriving at a scene of domestic violence treat the real fears of a battered wife too lightly—feeling, apparently, that the attack was simply the result of some family quarrel in which the law has no business interfering.

Experts maintain that long-term solutions to domestic violence must be based on preventative education, in which children learn that anger and conflict need not be channeled through violence. The United States, these observers believe, is a country in which a "tough guy" cult dominates social, political, and family life. Boys who grow up to be men in this atmosphere too easily convince themselves that wife beating is just another way of exhibiting masculinity and control.

In many cities, women's groups and other agencies have established shelters for battered wives. "But what we really need are shelters for the men—places to get their brains fixed," said a Seattle shelter operator.

Battlestar Discovery

is the media name for a military space shuttle launched in January 1985. The term is a parody of the old television series "Battlestar Galactica," which was about a military spaceship.

The space shuttle carried a $300 million spy satellite to a secret orbit in space. Details of the launch were kept hidden to thwart Soviet satellites which usually keep track of U.S. spacecraft.

The two-and-a-half ton satellite carried into orbit by Battlestar Discovery will orbit about twenty-two thousand miles above the earth. If it operates as anticipated, the satellite will travel at about the same speed as the earth and will be able to "see" through clouds and weather systems. Its high-resolution cameras are expected to provide, for the first time, continuous and detailed photo coverage of vast areas of the Soviet Union and China. The satellite's communication devices will be able to intercept a much wider range of telephone, microwave, and satellite transmissions than was previously possible.

The launch cost $31 million. Battlestar Discovery's crew included four NASA astronauts and a member of the Manned Space Flight Engineer Corps—an elite team of specialists being trained to operate military spacecraft.

B-1 Bomber

Rockwell International began developing the B-1 bomber about twenty years ago to replace the U.S. Air Force's B-52 Stratofortress, which experts predicted would become obsolete in the late 1980s.

The B-1 is huge, designed to carry more bombs and missiles (115,000 pounds) than any aircraft ever devised. It flies at 1,450 miles per hour and carries complex operational systems.

The Air Force planned to have 240 B-1s by 1985, but the Carter administration canceled the program in 1977. President Reagan resurrected the B-1 in 1981, when $1.8 billion was spent to produce the first fully operational prototype. In 1982, seven more B-1s were authorized by Congress, and in 1984 $6 billion was spent to add ten more bombers to the B-1 fleet.

Critics of the B-1 program say that the bomber is too expensive and difficult to maintain. Proponents, including President Reagan, believe the aircraft is essential to maintain U.S. strength at the bargaining table in arms control talks, primarily to offset the Soviet Union's ICBM superiority.

Bellwether,

a sheep that leads the entire flock, is a term used to describe a precinct (*see* Precinct), congressional district, or state which has a history of reflecting the voting patterns of the nation as a whole. Typically, a bellwether area has a population mix closely reflecting national demographics.

Bhopal,

India, a town 360 miles south of New Delhi, was the site in 1984 of history's worst industrial accident.

According to scientists investigating the disaster, a pint of water was the cause.

Dr. S. Varadarajan, in an official report of the events of December 2-3, 1984, said that water apparently seeped into an underground tank at the Union Carbide pesticide plant near Bhopal and triggered a powerful chemical reaction that cracked the tank's concrete shield.

The tank contained a deadly chemical called methyl isocyanate. When the tank ruptured, fifteen tons of the toxic substance were turned into a kind of plastic. Another thirty tons were released as gas, which spread quickly through Bhopal, killing twenty-five hundred people and injuring more than 100,000 others.

Biochip

is theoretically a man-made organism which would perform many computer system functions. Unlike computer chips made of silicon or other inorganic materials (see Microchip), the biochip will not be manufactured; it will be grown from living bacteria.

Development of a working biochip is the top priority of genetic engineering (see Genetic Engineering), research funded by the information-processing industry. If successful, these scientists will produce microprocessors ten million times more efficient than today's most powerful computers. Desk-top devices could store more information than today's mainframe processors.

Theoretically, the biochip would have several advantages over existing computer circuitry. Organic materials would be faster, smaller, and cheaper than the silicon chip. Malfunctioning biochips could "heal" themselves, dramatically reducing the need for repair or replacement.

Thousands of applications for the biochips have been envisioned. The chips might be connected to the human nervous system, to assume the functions of damaged eyes, ears, or vocal chords, to monitor and correct chemical imbalances, or to compensate for nerve or muscle dysfunctions. In industry, biochips could revolutionize robotics by controlling machines which could replace humans in high-risk jobs, such as fire-fighting or toxic-waste disposal.

Genetic engineers believe that the first working biochip could be completed by 1990.

Biofeedback

is a procedure in which electronic monitors are used to train people to control supposedly involuntary body functions such as heartbeat, blood pressure, brain waves, muscle contraction, and blood flow.

A form of therapy especially effective in the treatment of psychosomatic disorders and hypertension, biofeedback employs technology to demystify and popularize techniques used for centuries by practitioners of yoga.

Sensors attached to the body communicate physiological information to monitors, where it is displayed for the patient and therapist to see. Together, they work to gain conscious control of the data. Once control is established, the patient can direct the body to respond to pain or other disorders.

The use of biofeedback in treating migraine attacks is typical of contemporary applications. In 1972, researchers discovered that the end of a migraine attack is typically accompanied by a sharp increase in finger temperature. Teaching migraine sufferers to raise finger temperature has proved effective in eliminating migraine attacks or reducing their duration.

In this therapy, temperature sensors are attached to the fingers and linked to an electronic device which, in turn, produces a series of clicks. The clicks become faster as the finger temperature rises. The patient imagines holding fingers to a warm fire or holding a steaming cup of coffee in order to elevate finger temperature.

Biofeedback is currently popular as a means of reducing or counteracting emotional stress.

Black Muslims

are members of an American black Islamic sect.

The movement was founded in the early 1930s in Detroit by W. D. Fard, a fabric salesman. Fard's followers believed he had come to the United States from Mecca, the holy city of the Islamic religion. When Fard disappeared in 1934, Elijah Muhammad, an auto worker whose original name was Elijah Poole, became the leader of the Black Muslims. Muhammad called himself a "prophet and apostle" and claimed that he had spoken to God through Fard.

Muhammad preached a militant anti-integrationist philosophy, often referring to whites as "beasts" or "devils." He urged black self-reliance and complete separation from white society—even economically.

One of the best known Black Muslim leaders was the charismatic Malcolm X. He was assassinated in 1965, about a year after he left the movement and converted to traditional Islam.

Elijah Muhammad died in 1975. His son and successor, Wallace Muhammad, has rejected the movement's separatist position, urging a "new patriotism" and integration into mainstream American society. Wallace Muhammad advocates religious unification with world Muslims and mainstream Islam, and claims to be neither a prophet nor an apostle.

Black Muslims, conservative in dress and deportment, follow a strict moral code. The movement maintains a large network of businesses and operates its own schools. Total U.S. membership in the religious group is estimated to be between a quarter to a half million.

The separatist doctrine espoused so vigorously by Elijah Muhammad survives in a group which split from the Black Muslim movement a few years ago, the Nation of Islam, headed by the frequently outrageous Louis Farrakhan.

Farrakhan attracted national attention when he suggested that a black reporter should be killed after the reporter printed anti-Semitic remarks made by black presidential candidate Jesse Jackson.

Early in 1985, President Muammar Qaddafi spoke to a Nation of Islam gathering via satellite. Qaddafi urged black members of the U.S. armed forces to form their own army and overthrow their government. Farrakhan, while rejecting Quaddafi's suggestion, expressed admiration for the Libyan leader.

Bloc

describes a dynamic alliance of voters, legislators, or nations acting together to protect or promote some common interest.

Senators and congressmen representing agricultural states are referred to as the "farm bloc." The Soviet Union, its satellites, and close allies are called the "Soviet bloc" or the "Eastern bloc."

Blood Boosting,

or blood packing, is a technique used to increase the body's oxygen-carrying capacity of the blood. It has been employed by world-class athletes to increase endurance.

Several weeks before an important competition, about a quart of blood is taken from an athlete. The blood's red cells are removed and put in cold storage. Shortly in advance of the athlete's event, the red cells are reinfused. The increased oxygen-carrying capacity of the cells allows greater exertion of the muscles over an extended period of time. Tests have shown that blood boosting can increase endurance by as much as 25 percent in most athletes. Transfusions of someone else's red cells can have the same effect, but transfusion is dangerous, likely to bring on flu symptoms, hepatitis, or mononucleosis.

Seven members of the U.S. cycling team, including four medalists, "blood boosted" during the 1984 Olympic games in Los Angeles. The practice, used widely in Europe by cyclists and long-distance skiers, was not technically against Olympic rules, though it did violate Olympic policy. Most sports medicine experts consider blood boosting unethical.

Blue Chips,

named after the poker chips of greatest value, are the most secure U.S. stocks. These securities have a long history of good earnings, regardless of the condition of the rest of the economy, and generally have a long record of uninterrupted dividend payments. Blue-chip companies are leaders in their industries, with strong prospects for continued growth and profitability. IBM and AT&T are examples of blue-chip stocks favored by investors seeking low risks and stable returns.

Brookings Institute,

located in Washington, D.C., is a non-partisan "think tank" devoted to research in economics, governmental policy, and public affairs. According to its staff, the organization "seeks to provide independent analysis and criticism of public policy."

The institute's staff includes a group of respected social scientists who serve as a liaison between the academic world, where new knowledge is formulated, and the world of government, where this knowledge can be applied in laws, policies, and programs.

Established in 1927, the Brookings Institute is maintained primarily by private contributions, although it sometimes receives grants from government agencies. The main function of the institute is research designed to measure the impact of legislation on society.

Critics consider the Brookings Institute too liberal in its orientation and point out that many of the institute's staff members are former advisers to Democratic presidents.

Brunei

is a tiny (population 250,000), oil-rich nation on the northwest coast of Borneo. By most standards, it is the richest country in the world, with $75,000 in the bank for every man, woman, and child within its border.

There are virtually no taxes in Brunei. The government provides free health care, housing, and education for each of its citizens.

All this is made possible by oil and natural gas, and the cheerful benevolence of Sultan Hassanal Bolkiah, who owns most of the country. Early in 1984, Bolkiah completed the world's largest and most expensive palace: eighteen hundred lavishly furnished rooms overlooking the South China Sea.

Bubble Boy

is what the media called a twelve-year-old Texan kept alive until February 1984 in a large plastic bubble.

The boy, known only as David (at the request of his parents), suffered from Severe Combined Immune Deficiency Syndrome (CIDS), a condition that rendered his body completely defenseless against disease.

David's treatment, which required that he live in a sterile chamber encased in plastic, sparked controversy within the medical community.

Reverend Raymond Lawrence, a former staff member at the hospital where David was treated, said that doctors gave little thought to the consequences of life in isolation, forcing a form of "technocratic imperialism" upon the child. Lawrence claimed that all decisions affecting David's life in isolation were made to advance the cause of science, without regard for "the potential emotional, psychological, and spiritual—that is to say, human—implications of life in the bubble."

When Lawrence's remarks were published in the *Journal of the American Medical Association*, Dr. Drummond Rennie, professor of medicine and a senior contributing editor of the journal, replied that the medical profession was indeed worried about the ethical issues raised by the case. Rennie noted that David's parents, doctors, and nurses all maintained "very human" relationships with the boy and substantial efforts were made to make David's life as normal as possible. He participated in school programs, received counseling and religious instruction, and was, to the extent possible, included in medical decisions affecting his life.

Even so, Lawrence insisted, "No one has discussed the horror of his existence."

David died February 22, 1984, as a result of an antibody inadvertently introduced into his system during a bone marrow transplant four months earlier.

Bulimia,

also known as "binge-purge syndrome," is a severe eating disorder suffered by an estimated five million Americans. Bulimics gorge themselves with food, then immediately induce vomiting.

The typical bulimic is a young well-educated middle or upper class woman who suffers from severe depression, anxiety, and low self-esteem. They are often successful in a career and are usually perfectionists. Only 5 percent of bulimics are male.

Bulimia is Greek for "ox hunger." The disease is appropriately named. Bulimics consume incredible quantities of food—fifty thousand calories a day isn't unusual.

Probably the best known bulimic is film actress Jane Fonda, who said she had the disease from age twelve to thirty-five, a period she called "twenty-three years of agony," during which she stuffed herself constantly and vomited fifteen to twenty times a day.

In its most serious form, bulimia is an addiction that completely dominates the life of the sufferer. Sometimes fatal, bulimia causes severe esophagus problems, chemical imbalances, and swollen glands. Dental problems are common in bulimics, caused by stomach acid which strips enamel from the teeth.

The accounts of women suffering from the disease indicate that, for bulimics, food is a vital drug, a necessary escape mechanism. Bulimics go to extraordinary lengths to perpetuate the binge-purge cycle.

One bulimic became a prostitute to support her food

habit; another was $6,000 in debt to her supermarket; still another reported a $100 a week laxative habit.

The binge-purge behavior dates back to the Roman Empire, but bulimia wasn't identified as a disease until 1903. Doctors disagree about how to treat bulimia, which has been alternately characterized as a psychological addiction, the result of a hormone imbalance, the manifestation of severe depression, and bad habit. Antidepressant drugs, psychotherapy, and self-help groups have all been tried, with moderate success.

Camp David

is a rustic retreat for U.S. presidents and visiting world leaders located in the Catoctin Mountains of Maryland, about seventy miles northwest of Washington, D.C. The camp's site was chosen because its elevation provides relief from the capital's oppressive summer heat, and because of the natural security afforded by the surrounding terrain.

The compound, built in the mid-1930s by Depression-era laborers, includes a presidential office and residence (Aspen Lodge), quarters for staff and guests, a conference center (Laurel Lodge), a pitch-and-putt golf course, and a swimming pool. The camp site is heavily wooded, laced with winding trails, and thick with underbrush. Its rough-hewn moss green cabins look much the same as they did when built almost fifty years ago.

Franklin Delano Roosevelt was the first president to use the camp, in 1942. He called it Shangri-La, the name of the utopian mountain kingdom in James Hilton's *Lost Horizon*, and the mythical site from which American bombers launched raids on Tokyo at the end of World War II.

President Dwight D. Eisenhower named the retreat Camp David, for his grandson (who grew up to marry Julie Nixon).

Beginning with the 1943 Roosevelt–Churchill meeting, the camp has been the site for many international conferences

—such as the 1959 meeting between Eisenhower and Soviet premier Nikita Khrushchev, and the 1978 meeting of President Jimmy Carter, President Anwar el-Sadat of Egypt, and Prime Minister Menachem Begin of Israel. Together, Carter, Sadat, and Begin fashioned a major agreement which became known as the Camp David Accord. "The spirit of Camp David" is frequently used by the news media as a synonym for international cooperation or a willingness on the part of antagonistic governments to negotiate their differences. President Reagan, like his predecessors, hosts many meetings at Camp David.

Capital Gain

is what economists (and the Internal Revenue Service) call a profit realized in buying or selling almost any kind of property —securities, real estate, art, precious gems, etcetera.

Short-term capital gains are taxed at the same rate as regular income. To encourage investment, long-term capital gains—profits over a period of at least one year—are taxed at a rate substantially below the rate applied to regular income.

For example, if an investor in the 50 percent income tax bracket buys stocks for $5,000 and sells them six months later for $10,000, he must pay $2,500 in taxes. Had the same transaction occurred within an interval of a year between the purchase and the sale, the investor would have been taxed on only 40 percent of his capital gain and would owe the IRS only $1,000.

Capital Punishment—

the death penalty—allows the execution of a convicted criminal under direction of a court. Currently, U.S. law limits capital punishment to specific types of murder.

The United States has periodically reinforced the death

penalty since the nation's beginnings. Executions declined steadily between 1933 and 1967, and for ten years beginning in 1967, no one was executed in this country until Gary Gilmore was shot to death by a Utah State Prison firing squad in 1977.

The American Civil Liberties Union (ACLU) and other opponents of capital punishment tried in the early 1970s to eradicate the death penalty through persistent litigation. In 1972, the U.S. Supreme Court decided that the death penalty was indeed unconstitutional if handed out "capriciously," without clear nondiscriminating standards. Because most state laws were not sufficiently precise in defining when the death penalty should apply, the 1972 decision effectively outlawed executions. In 1976, the court clarified the capital punishment issue, allowing the death penalty in certain carefully defined types of murder—premeditated, cruel (torture), and murders committed in association with other felonies. The court ruled out capital punishment for rape because it considered the death penalty for this crime to be "cruel and unusual punishment"—too severe for the offense committed.

Opponents of capital punishment say that the death penalty is cruel and unusual punishment. There is no conclusive evidence, critics claim, that capital punishment deters potential murderers. The death penalty, according to its opponents, is frequently motivated by revenge, a motive not worthy of civilized law. Also, critics say, no matter how carefully laws are structured, the decision on who will die rests with human judges and juries—people with ingrained, unconscious prejudices which prevent the law from being applied uniformly.

Its supporters contend that capital punishment traditionally has been acceptable throughout civilized history, that it displays a regard for the sacred nature of human life, and that it is needed to fight violent crime. Proponents of the death penalty admit that evidence of its effectiveness as a deterrent is ambiguous, but believe that if it deters even one potential murder, it has served its purpose. Officials who favor capital punishment believe that the community has a moral right to demand the death penalty as an expression of outrage for the ultimate crime.

Over the past few years, executions have become more

frequent in the United States, where there are now about fourteen hundred death row inmates awaiting execution. A 1983 Supreme Court decision drastically shortened the appeals process in capital cases. Polls taken in 1984 indicate that about 72 percent of the public favors the death penalty, a considerable shift from attitudes of ten years earlier, when less than half approved of executions.

Carbohydrate Cravings

A study completed in 1985 at the Massachusetts Institute of Technology (MIT) indicates that about half of all obese people experience a physical craving for carbohydrates (sugars and starches).

According to MIT researchers, carbohydrate cravers grab a sweet or starchy snack when they feel irritable, distracted, or unable to concentrate. Carbohydrates are absorbed quickly into the blood and, through a complicated chain reaction, increase the brain's production of serotonin—a "message-carrying" chemical that influences mood and makes the craver calm and better able to concentrate.

Nutritionists analyzing the MIT study have suggested that carbohydrate snacks, eaten once a day, might satisfy mood-related cravings and help obese people afflicted with them to lose weight.

Caribbean Basin Initiative

is a package of tax and trade incentives designed to encourage investment in the Caribbean economy. The CBI authorizes economic aid for non-Communist Caribbean and Central American nations, provides duty-free status for most CBI member exports, and offers tax deductions to U.S. businessmen in CBI countries. After the Grenada invasion and installation of a government friendly to the United States, CBI benefits were extended to that country.

Caucus,

derived from the name of an eighteenth-century social-political club, means "closed meeting" and has several slightly different applications.

During election campaigns, caucuses are part of the nomination process in several states. Party members meet at the precinct level to agree upon candidates.

A caucus is also a faction within a political party that meets regularly to formulate positions on various issues. The Democratic Party has a Black Caucus, a Women's Caucus, a Farm Caucus, and several more. Some party leaders complain that this proliferation of caucuses prevents the Democrats from presenting a united front on any issue. One Democrat claimed he wouldn't be surprised to see a Left-Handed Midget Caucus in the near future. Republicans have caucuses too, though fewer than the Democrats. Republicans call their caucus-like factions "conferences."

At the beginning of each session of Congress, party caucuses are held to organize day-to-day business. Party floor leaders and whips (see Whip) are chosen and key positions on committees are distributed.

Central Intelligence Agency (CIA)

was established in 1947 by the National Security Council to coordinate all military and political espionage in the United States and wherever the United States has interests. Ostensibly, the CIA exists to advise the National Security Council on security issues; to coordinate the intelligence efforts of all government departments and the armed services for the president to correlate, evaluate, and distribute intelligence to government agencies; and to undertake "other security tasks."

Exactly what constitutes these other security tasks is vaguely defined in the CIA charter, but historically these tasks have included financing Radio Free Europe, training anti-Communist guerrillas in Latin America, helping governments friendly to the United States stifle "counterinsurgency" (see Counterinsurgency), and, it has been charged, providing trained killers for allies.

Charisma

is a combination of attractiveness, personal charm, and sincerity—a special quality that captures the popular imagination and inspires allegiance, even devotion.

People who can't define charisma know it when they see it. A politician with charisma can attract a following outside his party and be popular with large groups who don't entirely agree with his policies.

Chile,

an eighteen-hundred-mile strip in South America between the Andes mountains and the Pacific Ocean, is, in the view of many experts, on the verge of social explosion.

In 1973, the current Chilean President Augusto Pinochet led a bloody military coup which deposed Marxist Salvador Allende. Evidence suggests that the U.S. Central Intelligence Agency (see CIA) actively participated in the overthrow.

Pinochet, upon taking office, promised free elections, but they have not taken place. Political opponents, convinced that

Pinochet planned to rule Chile indefinitely, organized protests beginning in 1983, and the country has been in a state of siege ever since. Pinochet's military government exercises virtually unlimited powers of arrest, censorship, search and seizure. More than seven hundred critics of the government have been exiled to remote regions of Chile. It is not known if they are alive or dead.

In addition to mounting political unrest, Chile is in the midst of a severe recession caused by a sharp decline in the value of copper, its chief export.

Observers feel that unless democratic reforms are initiated, Chile's Communist Party will exploit political and economic conditions to gain control of the government. President Reagan has warned Chilean leaders that their repressive policies are increasing Communism's attractiveness to the nation's people, but the United States has almost no influence on Pinochet, having cut off all significant aid to Chile in the late 1970s in protest of human rights violations.

Chilean rebels are hoping to enlist other socialist countries in their attempt to oust Pinochet's government. They envision a scenario similar to the Sandinista (see Sandinista) takeover of Nicaragua (see Nicaragua), in which military aid from Cuba and the USSR played a significant role.

Violence has erupted intermittently in Chile since May 1983, but as of early 1985, the government saw no threat of a successful revolution. Only a few hundred guerrillas are thought to be active full time, supported by about five thousand sympathizers.

Coal Gasification

is a process for converting coal to gases which can be used as fuel and in the manufacture of several chemicals and fertilizers. Products of the process could replace natural gas and petroleum.

The coal gasification process uses high temperatures and

extreme pressure to "crack" coal carbon molecules into lighter molecules from which synthetic gas can be extracted and converted to methane—a good substitute for natural gas.

In the early 1980s, energy experts realized that natural gas reserves were diminishing and suggested that coal gasification experiments begin in earnest as part of the U.S. government's "synfuel" (see Synfuel) effort—a research and development plan that, so far, has gotten almost nowhere.

If the coal gasification process can be perfected (it's still in the experimental stage) and implemented on a major scale, some experts believe it could allow pollution-free use of all grades of coal (plentiful in the United States)—even those high-sulfur coals now considered unusable because of the pollutants they generate. (See Acid Rain)

Coalition

is a fusion of various political elements to achieve a specific goal, and is often temporary. In countries having a number of political parties, coalitions are often necessary to form a working legislative majority. In the United States, coalitions form within the two major parties, and sometimes across party boundaries.

During the 1984 presidential campaign, for example, candidate Jesse Jackson tried to assemble what he called a "rainbow coalition"—an organization committed to the underprivileged and to the unification of people from all racial and political backgrounds.

Coattail Effect

is a theory which holds that a popular candidate at the top of an election ticket can sweep other candidates into office who, on their own, might not have won. Abraham Lincoln first popularized the phrase in 1848.

The theory is based on the assumption that many voters prefer to vote a straight ticket. Sometimes the coattail effect theory seems valid, other times not. Lyndon Johnson's 1964 landslide helped his party win a sizeable gain in the House of Representatives; but Reagan's mammoth 1984 victory didn't result in any substantial change in the composition of the Congress.

Parties frequently design their campaigns to encourage the coattail effect, placing attractive candidates strategically throughout the ballot and pushing for a "straight ticket" vote.

Codeine

is the key ingredient of some seventy million prescriptions filled each year in the United States. The drug, used in pain relievers and cough medicines, is derived from the poppy, the same plant that produces morphine, opium, and the poppy seeds used to garnish bread, rolls, and bagels.

Most of the codeine used in the United States comes from India, where it is manufactured by government-authorized companies. Years ago, cough syrups containing codeine were sold over-the-counter and used by some as the source of a cheap high. Codeine is still abused, but to a much lesser extent.

Communications Satellite Corporation (COMSAT)

is a joint U.S. government—private enterprise organization created in 1962 to build, launch, and maintain a system of communications satellites in space. Several hundred private communications companies were involved in Communications Satellite Corporation.

In 1963, companies and governments of eighteen nations agreed to participate in an expansion of COMSAT operations, which led to INTELSAT, the International Telecommunications Satellite Consortium.

Today, INTELSAT has 109 member nations which, in cooperation with private firms, operate global satellite relays for telephone, telegraph, radio, and television communications.

Comparable Worth

is the label supporters have given the concept of equal pay for jobs which have the same value to industry or society.

According to a survey released in 1985 by the National Committee on Pay Equity (a coalition of unions, women's organizations, and civil rights groups), four out of five working Americans support the comparable worth concept—despite the avalanche of costly lawsuits likely to be filed should the proposal become law.

Although only beginning, debates over how various jobs should be ranked on a comparable worth scale are already becoming emotional and heated. Many supporters of the concept argue that wages in fields dominated by women, such as nursing, teaching, and clerical professions, are depressed in value and should be adjusted to match pay levels existing in male-oriented jobs requiring comparable skills, training, and responsibilities.

Critics of the concept see a comparable worth statute leading to a hopeless tangle of endless litigation and say that the real solution to the disparity between men's and women's salaries will level off over time as more women advance to higher paid jobs.

Conglomerate

is a giant corporation made up of several smaller companies.

A product of the 1960s, conglomerates were created by transportation and electronics companies looking for ways to become less dependent upon their traditional markets, which they considered too vulnerable to seasonal or cyclical pressure.

It became common, as conglomerates grew, to find the same firm involved in interests as diversified as motels, artificial limbs, motion pictures, mail-order houses, and insurance.

Investors originally liked the idea of diversified conglomerates offering a chance for growth in so many areas. Conglomerate stock commanded good prices.

By 1970, conglomerates began to lose favor on Wall Street. Too many had overdiversified, borrowed too much, and engaged in peculiar accounting practices that masked insolvency. The value of conglomerate stocks fell, and many of the large corporations were reduced in size or dismantled entirely. By 1984, only about forty conglomerates remained in business.

Over the next five years, conglomerates are expected to return to prominence. Financial experts point out that in pieces these corporate octopuses are worth considerably more than they are whole. A rash of conglomerate dissolutions is anticipated, and estimating the "break up" value of a company that can be sold in pieces is expected to become an important Wall Street exercise.

Constitutional Amendment

is a change in, or an addition to, the nation's governing charter.

Proposed amendments must be ratified by three-fourths of the states within a specified time frame (usually seven years). Thousands of constitutional amendments have been proposed, but only twenty-six have been adopted. The amendment procedure has occasionally been criticized because it allows a minority to block the wishes of the majority.

The Reagan administration claims to favor two amendment proposals—one to outlaw abortion, the other to allow prayer in public schools.

Consumer Price Index (CPI)

is a gauge used to measure the cost of living for an average U.S. consumer. The CPI is often called the "cost of living" index.

To prepare the CPI, the Labor Department studies what typical households are buying and tries to determine the percentage of the family budget spent on housing, utilities, gas, clothing, transportation, entertainment, and incidentals. The average food budget is examined in even greater detail to create an average "market basket" containing the appropriate proportions of meat, eggs, fresh produce, cereals, cleaning supplies, etcetera.

These typical consumer expenditures form a base which, each month, is reviewed to find the rate at which prices are moving and in which direction.

The CPI is used for the "indexing" required in many labor contracts and the Social Security program. Indexing adjusts worker salaries and social security benefits to reflect the cost of living increases shown in the CPI. Beginning in 1985, income tax rates, brackets, and deductions will also be indexed.

Contadora Group

is the name taken by Central and South American diplomats seeking to diffuse tensions in the region.

The Contadora group includes representatives from Mexico, Venezuela, Colombia, and Panama. Since 1983, Contadora has offered dozens of proposals for peace in El Salvador, Nicaragua, Honduras, and Guatemala. (*See* El Salvador, Nicaragua, Honduras, and Guatemala)

These proposals generally include non-intervention in another country's affairs, amnesty for rebel groups, openness in government, and establishment of human-rights policies.

As of early 1985, Contadora efforts to bring about peace negotiations have had no tangible success.

Contras

are Central American guerrilla (*see* Guerrilla) forces opposed to the leftist Sandinist (*see* Sandinista) government of Nicaragua (*see* Nicaragua) and dedicated to its overthrow.

Because the Sandinistas characterize their rise to power as "the revolution," the opposition has adopted the name contra—counter-revolutionaries.

There are two major contra groups, the Democratic Revolutionary Alliance (Arde) based in Costa Rica, and the Nicaraguan Democratic Force (FDN), which operates from Honduras.

The Reagan administration, believing that the Sandinist government represents a dangerous communist presence in Central America, supports the contras, whom President Reagan has called "democratic freedom fighters."

Administration bills which would have supplied military and economic aid to the contras were defeated in the U.S. House of Representatives in April 1985. Republican leaders sought to revive these measures in early May after Nicaraguan president Daniel Ortega traveled to Moscow and received Soviet pledges of assistance. Several legislators who had voted against aid to the contras said Ortega's trip embarrassed them.

Corporate Income Tax,

a federal tax levied against the annual net income of all corporations, is considered a tax on the privilege of doing business as a legally chartered corporation.

Currently, corporate tax rates begin at 17 percent (of the first $25,000 in income) and escalate to 46 percent (of all net income over $100,000).

The corporate income tax is probably the most complex tax and has generated considerable controversy over what constitutes "net income" and legitimate expenses.

The tax, critics say, fosters "double taxation," because the government taxes a company's profits twice—first through the corporate income tax, and again when shareholders' dividends are taxed through the personal-income-tax structure. President Reagan, early in his first term, proposed the abolition of the corporate income tax, which, he said, reduced the profit incentive. Others lament the corporate tax system's incredible maze of deductions, credits, and loopholes.

Costa Rica,

a Central American nation located between Panama and Nicaragua, is considered strategically important by the United States because of its proximity to the Panama Canal.

A republic since 1848, Costa Rica has had one of the most consistently democratic governments in Central America. Until the Nicaraguan crisis, Costa Rica was extremely friendly to the United States. Now there are factions within Costa Rica expressing concern that close ties with the U.S. could threaten the nation's neutrality and bring war with Nicaragua. (See Nicaragua)

In a May 1984 radio broadcast, President Reagan charged that Nicaragua's Sandinist government (see Sandinista), "in partnership with Cuba and the Soviet Union," was supporting aggression against Costa Rica. Reagan claimed that Nicaraguan agents had been caught in Costa Rica supervising terrorist attacks. Calling Nicaragua's contention that Costa Rica threatened its security "a lie," Reagan noted that Costa Rica "doesn't even have an army." (It does have a national guard of six thousand.)

Later in 1984, twenty to thirty thousand Costa Ricans marched in opposition to their government's request for $7.6 million in U.S. military aid, contending that the aid would jeopardize Costa Rican neutrality and Central American peace.

Counterinsurgency

is a CIA term for military actions taken against grass-roots guerrilla movements (usually Marxist) by governments friendly to the United States. When guerrillas are fighting for the overthrow of governments hostile to the United States, counterinsurgency is called violent, brutal repression.

Covert Activities

are intelligence initiatives usually taken without the explicit approval of any government agency.

Over the past decade, the CIA has used covert activities in elections held in other countries, participated in or condoned political assassinations, and fought—or helped others fight— wars in which the United States had not officially been involved.

In 1984, covert activities of the CIA, which led to controversy and sparked outrage in the United States and abroad, included involvement in the mining of Nicaraguan harbors, and distribution of "terror manuals" to anti-Marxist guerrillas.

Creationists

believe that the biblical account of the earth's genesis is literally accurate. The fundamentalist Christian movement promotes creationism as scientific fact and, in some Southern states, has influenced legislators to require that creationism be given "equal treatment" in schools.

Scientists, including many Christians, point out that overwhelming evidence indicates that the earth evolved slowly, over hundreds of millions of years (the theory of evolution—proposed by Charles Darwin). Creationists argue that the theory of evolution is an unproven, scientific supposition.

Scientists, disgusted and alarmed that creationism still has proponents, have gone to almost absurd lengths to disprove creationist doctrine. One physicist presented a detailed refutation of the Bible's account of the Great Flood, attempting to show how impossibly huge an ark would have to have been to carry two of each species.

Scientists who are also Christians maintain that the theory of evolution (and other scientific thought) does not deny a Supreme Being was involved in the earth's creation, only that it took God considerably more than a week to finish his work.

Cruise Missiles

are medium- to long-range nuclear weapons resembling small pilotless aircraft. Controlled by an onboard navigation system which requires no guidance after launch, these missiles are able to cruise long distances at low altitudes.

To find its target, a cruise missile follows a flight path which has been programmed into its navigational mechanisms. Using radar, the cruise missile "compares" the terrain it is flying over with a digital map in its guidance program. The missile is thus able to fly itself, up to 2,000 miles.

The most advanced cruise missiles to date are the US Tomahawk, designed for naval launch, and the ALCM (Air Launched Cruise Missile).

NATO agreements to deploy cruise missiles in Western Europe led to many months of anti-nuclear demonstrations in the United States and abroad.

Cryobiology

is the study of the effects of extreme cold on living tissue. Scientists working in this field are trying to determine how to freeze and store healthy organs for use in transplants later, and attempting to destroy diseased tissue through the use of extremely cold probes (cryosurgery). Cryobiology is a legitimate science and should not be confused with cryonics, a highly speculative theory which suggests that ailing humans be frozen and thawed out years later when a cure for their affliction is available.

Cyanide

is a fast-acting, extremely deadly poison. Whether it is inhaled or ingested, cyanide affects the respiratory system, preventing the body from using oxygen.

Certain forms of cyanide are useful in mining, plastics production, and several other industries. Wastes contaminated with cyanide are causing serious disposal problems in a number of industrial areas throughout the United States. Officers of an Illinois company were recently indicted for murder when company workers died from cyanide poisoning, allegedly due to flagrant violations of safety regulations governing the use and disposal of the chemical.

Cyclosporine

is an antirejection drug that suppresses the immune system's reaction to foreign tissue without destroying its ability to combat infection.

The new drug was highly successful in 1984, greatly enhancing the success rate of organ transplants. Surgeons have already mastered the mechanics of the transplant process. Typically, however, the patient's body rebelled against the new organ. Before cyclosporine, antirejection drugs too often stripped the patient's body of its defenses against even minor bacterial infections.

Unfortunately, cyclosporine has one major drawback. It has been reported that the drug could cause long-term kidney damage if given in large doses continuously.

Damitol,

a toy tranquilizer which spoofs the dozens of real anti-stress medications on the market, "relaxed" American pursestrings to the tune of $500,000 in 1984.

A gag gift made of cinnamon candy, Damitol pills sell for $3.95 a bottle in novelty stores and gift shops. Invented by Steve Merritt of Ann Arbor, Michigan, Damitol is a gimmick *à la* "pet rock" that guarantees "instant relief from the physical and emotional traumas induced by overbearing bosses, insensitive spouses, belligerent children, obnoxious brothers-in-law, defective appliances, catatonic lovers. . . ." In short, Damitol is "effective" in any crisis, an all-purpose antidote to the travails of modern life.

For 1985, Damitol's distributor promises Divorce Formula Damitol and, for tax-time headaches, an Extra Strength 1040 Formula version.

Delegates

attend a political party's nominating convention and participate in selecting the nominee who will represent the party as its candidate for president.

Rules for delegate selection vary from one state to another, from one political party to another, and from one election year to another. Until fairly recently, delegate selection was a closed process tightly controlled by professional politicians, almost all of whom were white, male, and middle class. The rules have become increasingly liberalized since 1968, when a powerful grass-roots movement began to advocate that more blacks, women, Hispanics, and poor people be allowed to take part in the nomination process.

Two basic forms of delegate selection exist—the primary election and the more traditional party caucus (*see* Caucus).

The caucus method is still employed in Iowa, Maine, and Michigan. In the late winter or early spring, people interested in becoming delegates attend township party meetings, or caucuses. At the meetings, those seeking delegate positions campaign on behalf of the presidential candidates they support, and the party members attending the caucus vote for the delegates they prefer. Those selected later go through an elimination vote at the county caucus level, and a final selection of delegates is made at a state caucus.

In other states, people seeking to become delegates must win a party primary election in the spring. Getting on the ballot usually requires the would-be delegate to collect several thousand signatures on a petition endorsing his or her candidacy. Since dozens of persons may collect enough signatures to have their names printed on the ballot, only those winning the largest vote totals go on to become delegates.

Regardless of the selection method, the number of delegates each state sends to its party conventions is proportional to the size of the state's electoral vote (*see* Electoral College).

Most persons seeking to become delegates pledge themselves to support a particular presidential candidate, since the candidate's popularity, name recognition, and campaign organization are the most important factors in helping the potential delegate to win elections. Running as a delegate "at large," i.e., without a commitment to support a candidate, is very difficult and usually succeeds only if the delegate has strong name recognition on his or her own or has become identified as the supporter of a popular cause.

When the first ballot is taken at the nominating convention, delegates traditionally vote for the candidate they had previously pledged to support. If no candidate receives a majority on the first ballot, however, delegates are free to switch their vote to a person they believe to be more promising.

In addition to delegates picked in caucuses and primaries, each party traditionally sets aside a certain percentage of its delegates for important party figures who automatically become delegates *ex officio*, or by virtue of their office. Big-city mayors, U.S. senators and representatives, and certain powerful aldermen, county commissioners, and state legislators historically hold these seats.

Deregulation,

also called "regulatory reform," is a policy designed to relax or remove government controls imposed upon private enterprise and individuals.

Regulation efforts fall into four general categories: health, safety, environment, and economy. Attempts at deregulation have been successful primarily in the economic area.

Deregulation proponents insist that a loosening of government rules would reduce the cost of most goods and services. Opponents insist that government supervision of many industries is essential for the protection of the public.

Under President Carter, the airline industry was deregulated in 1978. While the Federal Aviation Administration continues to enforce regulations governing airline safety, the Civil Aeronautics Board lost its authority to restrict the routes the airlines fly and the fares they charge. New carriers entered some existing markets while traditional carriers withdrew from routes they no longer found remunerative. Intense competition brought fares to new lows.

In 1980, a similar reform came to the nation's freight railroad industry when the Staggers Deregulation Act was passed. The railroads no longer had to file applications with the Interstate Commerce Commission in order to revise their rates. Like other businesses, they could raise or lower rates at will, quote special rates to favored customers, and keep their rates secret from their competitors. They were allowed to close money-losing branch lines. For the first time in ninety years the railroads began to grow healthy.

The Reagan administration has made a concentrated effort to purge "meddlesome" regulations, and to eliminate—or reduce the power of—the government agencies which enforce them.

A Task Force on Regulatory Relief was formed in January 1981 to review and revoke as many regulations as it could. When the task force disbanded two years later, it claimed to have saved U.S. industry $150 billion over the next ten years and announced victory over "runaway regulation."

Détente

is a French word meaning to relax. In foreign affairs the word suggests an easing of tensions between nations, especially between the United States and the Soviet Union. Détente was first used this way in 1955 by President Eisenhower. Twenty-two years later, President Jimmy Carter redefined it as "progress toward peace."

The heyday of détente was the early 1970s when U.S. and USSR leaders held a series of summit conferences that led to significant arms control and trade agreements. But détente gave way to tension, beginning with the Soviet invasion of Afghanistan (see Afghanistan) in 1980, followed by the U.S. boycott of the Moscow Olympics, a U.S. embargo on grain shipments to the Soviet Union, and the destruction of a Korean commercial airliner which ventured into Soviet airspace.

Many respected foreign-affairs experts are proponents of détente and feel that a suspicious, adversarial relationship between the United States and the Soviet Union increases the risk of nuclear war. Conservatives, however, attack policies implemented in the wake of détente as "sellouts . . . give-aways." According to one critic, détente is "like going to a wife-swapping party and coming home alone."

Until recently, President Reagan has shown no interest in reviving détente, preferring a confrontational approach in dealing with the USSR. Three Soviet leaders have come to power and died without ever having met Reagan.

The United States will negotiate with the Soviet Union, Reagan aides have promised, but only because "the adoption of a muscular stance worldwide makes it possible for us to negotiate from a position of strength."

Diablo Canyon,

a nuclear power plant located on the central coast of California, has been a source of controversy since its construction began in 1981.

The plant at Avila Beach, California, is only three miles away from a major offshore earthquake fault. Opponents of the plant fought its licensing on the grounds that Diablo Canyon's owner, Pacific Gas and Electric Co., does not have an emergency plan for dealing with a simultaneous nuclear accident and earth tremor.

On August 18, 1984, The Nuclear Regulatory Commission (see NRC) issued a license for the plant to begin full operations, noting that the chances for a simultaneous earth tremor and nuclear accident were too small to be significant.

Shortly afterwards, the San Luis Obispo Mothers for Peace filed a lawsuit challenging the NRC's decision. The U.S. Court of Appeals upheld Diablo Canyon's licensing, but noted, however, that the failure to consider earth tremor precautions "exhibited a substantial lapse in rational decision making."

Discount Rate

is the interest rate that a nation's central bank—such as the Federal Reserve Bank (see Federal Reserve System)—charges on loans to commercial banks. This rate affects the interest charged by commercial banks to corporate customers. Higher discount rates cause banks to raise their interest rates, which tends to discourage borrowing while lower discount rates have the opposite effect.

Dollar Diplomacy,

or "economic imperialism," is the use of economic, political, or military power to further the foreign business interests of a nation's large corporations.

Anti-American governments, especially in Latin America, charge that U.S. foreign policy is based on dollar diplomacy. Those leveling the charges contend that the United States is colonizing the labor forces and raw materials of foreign lands, exploiting nations in which people are starving.

State Department officials reject the dollar diplomacy charge, pointing out that U.S. firms operating in foreign lands usually do so at the invitation of foreign governments and that the income generated by American businesses abroad is shared with foreign workers.

Double Dipping

is the practice of collecting two government salaries, a government salary *and* a pension, or two government pensions. The checks come one on top of the other, like two scoops of pistachio atop a "double dip" ice cream cone.

A typical double-dipping situation occurs when a member of the military serves long enough to qualify for a service pension, retires, and then obtains a civilian job in government. More unusual, and generally frowned upon, are cases in which an individual is on the payroll of both a state and county agency.

Dungeons and Dragons

is a free-form, role-playing game in which players become medieval characters in search of adventure and treasure. At the start of each Dungeons and Dragons game, each player assumes a personal (cleric, fighter, magic user, or thief) and a physical type (human, elf, gnome, dwarf, etc.). Personality traits, acquired through rolls of the dice, govern what a character can and can't do. A "dungeonmaster," the only person who knows the game's entire plot, sends the characters off after treasure, revenge, or some other goal. Along the way, characters meet monsters, mazes, and pitfalls. They may be plagued by insanity, sadomasochism, or homicidal or suicidal curses. How players fare depends on the dungeonmaster's assessment of their character's abilities.

Critics of the game, a coalition of psychiatrists, Christian fundamentalists, and parents, charge that Dungeons and Dragons can lure young people into violence, the occult, insanity, and even suicide. "People have died because of this game," said Dr. Thomas Radecki, a University of Illinois psychiatrist. "Players actually step into this other life so many hours a week —into a world of medieval witchcraft and violence. The game teaches players to think violence is a useful tool."

Fundamentalist preachers have called Dungeons and Dragons "Satan's game." In 1982, a Vermont teenager killed himself after a "suicidal mania" curse was placed on his Dungeons and Dragons character. Two years later, a twelve-year-old shot his brother and then himself, allegedly acting on a death pact that was part of the game.

Dungeons and Dragons has over four million enthusiasts in the United States. The company that markets the game, TSR, Inc., vigorously defends it, claiming Dungeons and Dragons stimulates creativity and problem-solving skills, and promotes cooperation rather than competition.

"It's improvisational theater around a table," said a TSR spokesperson. "We've role-played all our lives. We have Walt Disney, *The Wizard of Oz, Star Wars.* Kids very distinctly understand the difference between fantasy and reality."

According to TSR executives, the company has a strict code of ethics which it applies to all game situations and plots. Evil is never to be shown in an attractive light. Excessive gore, rape, perversion, and disrespect for authentic religions are not permitted.

Replying to the charge that Dungeons and Dragons provokes suicide, the TSR spokesperson said: "When someone's pointing a finger at the game, we always find severe problems in the victim's personal life. Anything can trigger tragedy if there's a deep underlying problem."

Dungeons and Dragons players admit that they sometimes get wrapped up in their characters and become depressed or angry when the character dies, but they reject the notion that this caused "normal" players to end up crazy or dead.

In what might be considered an indirect response to critics, Dungeons and Dragons instructional booklets contain this advice: "Players are not characters! It is important to remember that the player and the character are two different persons. The more the two are kept apart, the better your games will be."

Early Retirement

The number of U.S. men leaving the work force between the ages of thirty-five and sixty-four has doubled since 1970. One-third of male workers now stop working before the traditional retirement age of sixty-five. The increase in early retirements is attributed to pressure from younger workers to "make room," attractive "early out" incentives offered by employers trying to reduce labor costs, and an increase in working wives.

Many labor experts are concerned about the trend toward early retirement, saying it results in a significant economic loss to the nation. According to a study done in New York City, an estimated $235 million in Social Security benefits would have been saved if half the city's "early dropouts" had stayed on the job another year. (These workers would also have paid income taxes on earnings of about $600 million.)

Some economists have suggested that U.S. companies had better start changing their policies to hold on to older workers, at least on a part-time basis. The U.S. labor force is decreasing significantly, these economists claim, and by the end of the 1980s there could be significant shortages in many professions.

The American Association of Retired Persons reports that two-thirds of early retirees are happy with their decision to leave the work force.

El Salvador,

named for "Jesus the Savior," is the smallest (8,268 square miles) and most densely populated (an estimated six million by 1985) republic in Central America. Its people are *mestizos*, of mixed Indian and European ancestry. Most of them are poor, living in urban and rural slums.

El Salvador achieved newsworthy status in 1980 when a small band of Marxist guerrillas launched a civil war in opposition to El Salvador's military government. Critics of American foreign policy, fearing American involvement, likened the war to another Vietnam.

Despite extensive American military and economic aid, the Salvadoran government has thus far been unable to defeat the guerrillas (see Guerrillas), who themselves have failed to gain control of the country, although they have managed to destroy its economy. Journalists who have returned from El Salvador point out that the majority of its citizens have little interest in supporting either the government or the rebels, although they fear attacks from both sides.

The Reagan administration contends that the guerrillas remain active because they continue to be armed and supplied by the Soviet Union and Cuba, by way of the Sandinist (see

Sandinista) government of neighboring Nicaragua (*see* Nicaragua).

Further, the administration fears that the continuing war in El Salvador is part of a campaign to spread communism throughout Central America. "I believe that the government of El Salvador is on the front line in a battle really aimed at the heart of the Western Hemisphere and eventually at us," President Reagan has said.

Administration opponents in Congress, although willing to support El Salvador, charge that the Salvadoran government is repressive and tolerates the activities of "death squads," which roam the countryside murdering suspected guerrilla sympathizers.

The controversy over El Salvador has abated somewhat since the election of Christian Democrat José Napoleón Duarte as president. Duarte has made substantial efforts to form a coalition government. He is viewed by many as a moderate committed to reforms which will better the quality of life in El Salvador and thus reduce popular support for the guerrillas. Duarte's efforts to initiate peace talks with leftist (*see* Political Spectrum) rebels have been complicated by a coalition of conservatives in the National Assembly and the army with its traditional independence from presidential control.

Electoral College

is a group of 538 representatives who, under the Constitution, are the only persons legally qualified to elect the president and vice-president of the United States.

Under Article II, section 1, paragraph 2 of the Constitution, the legislature of each state appoints electors equal in number to the total of the state's two senators plus all its representatives. After the presidential election, usually in December, each state's electors meet at their state capital and cast their votes for president and vice-president. The results of the various state votes are then communicated to the President of the U.S. Senate (the vice-president of the United States). Only after the vice-president has officially tallied the votes and announced them to the Senate does the United States have a legally chosen president-elect.

Since the Civil War, members of the electoral college have nearly always cast their votes to reflect the outcome of the popular vote for president in their states. An exception occurred in Alabama in 1968: although a clear majority of the state's voters chose Richard M. Nixon, one elector nevertheless cast his ballot for Alabama Governor George C. Wallace. Two presidents (Rutherford B. Hayes in 1876 and Benjamin Harrison in 1888) have won the presidency in the electoral college despite failing to win the popular vote.

The origin of the electoral college was the so-called "Great Compromise" struck between the populous states and the frontier states in their efforts to establish a common Constitution. One early plan—having the President elected by the state legislatures—would have made the president subservient to Congress. Another plan—direct popular election—would have given too much power to the large states.

Employee Stock Ownership Plan (ESOP)

operates on a simple premise: if employees are given ownership of a large block of stock in the company for which they work, growth in corporate loyalty, improved labor-management relations, increased productivity, and higher profits will result.

According to the National Center for Employee Ownership, over ten million workers now participate in more than seven thousand ESOPs. In 1976, there were only 843 ESOPs available to about 500,000 employees.

The phenomenal growth in employee ownership has been carefully nurtured by Congress, which has provided several attractive tax incentives to corporations offering ESOPs. Corporate contributions to an ESOP are tax deductible, as are cash dividends paid to ESOPs. Banks and other financial institutions that lend money to ESOPs pay income tax on only half of the interest they collect.

In several cases, employees have used ESOPs to save their jobs. Borrowing money through the plan, they then use the funds to buy and operate plants that the parent company had planned to close.

Recently, an ESOP was used as part of a strategy to counteract an unwanted corporate takeover. Phillips Petroleum agreed to create a $1.5 billion ESOP to place about one-third of the company's stock in the hands of employees in an effort to counter a "hostile" takeover attempt. The company anticipated that employees would vote their shares against any potentially job-threatening takeover. A U.S. District Court judge ruled, however, that foiling hostile takeovers was not the original purpose of ESOPs and represented an abuse of the plan.

Entrapment,

in criminal law, is a defense which maintains that the conduct of law-enforcement officials enticed or persuaded a defendant into doing something illegal—something he or she would not have done under normal circumstances.

Former automobile company president John De Lorean successfully used the entrapment defense to gain acquittal on cocaine trafficking charges in 1984. De Lorean's lawyers were able to convince a jury that FBI agents, taking advantage of De Lorean's desperate need for money (to keep his company afloat), induced De Lorean into a cocaine purchase that he never would have considered had the agents not suggested it.

Between 1978 and 1980, the "ABSCAM" investigation resulted in the conviction of seven U.S. legislators and several local and state officials for bribery, conspiracy, and other charges. In the ABSCAM investigation, FBI agents posed as an Arab sheik and his associates. Agents offered government officials bribes and then videotaped the transactions which resulted.

Critics of the methods used by the FBI in ABSCAM charged entrapment, but few of the accused used the entrapment defense because it required admission that an illegal act had occurred. In two major cases where entrapment was used as a defense, the court ruled that the FBI had stayed within legal limits.

Ergonomics

is an engineering approach in which the entire work environment (machinery, furniture, lighting, and acoustics) is designed to complement human abilities and limitations. Its principles were first employed during World War II to counteract problems which arose due to mismatches of men and equipment. (Planes crashed, whales were bombed with depth charges, and soldiers got stuck in tanks.)

Ergonomic engineers try to provide office and factory environments that workers can operate in comfortably. Their objective is to eliminate monotony, fatigue, noise, vibration, and other distractions that reduce productivity. Ergonomic engineers study how workers use existing equipment to do their jobs. After determining what should be improved in a work setting (a computer screen too bright, or tilted at an angle which promotes neck cramps, for instance), ergonomic experts typically build a test site to evaluate the effectiveness of corrective measures.

In the ergonomical perfect work setting, a worker's tools and machinery are laid out within easy reach. Specially contoured furniture prevents muscle strain, and work moves forward at a steady but not tiring pace.

Ethiopia,

an east African nation of nearly forty million people—with a per capita income of less than fifty cents a day—may lose 20 percent of its population to starvation by the end of 1985.

A severe drought has afflicted Ethiopia since 1981. The lack of water, together with overgrazing, the indiscriminate leveling of forests, and destructive agricultural practices, has brought the two thousand-year-old nation the worst famine in over a decade.

During a six-month period beginning in August 1984, the United States and other Western countries shipped 500,000 tons of food to Ethiopia. Visitors and officials of world relief organizations calculated that at least another 500,000 tons was needed.

Relief camps all over northern Ethiopia, where the worst famine has occurred, are full. Ten to twenty thousand people live in each camp, most without shelter, existing on daily rations unlikely to include much more than a cup of milk and a fortified biscuit. During January 1985, in a camp near Bati, fifty Ethiopians died each day, which required the services of thirty-five full-time grave diggers.

The epidemic starvation is complicated by a civil war being waged in the provinces of Tigre and Eritrea, where four million are in desperate need of food. The rebels seeking independence have been fighting the government since 1975.

Ethiopia's government—a Marxist military dictatorship ruled by Lieutenant Colonel Mengistu Haile Mariam—was sharply criticized throughout the world for delaying food shipments to rebel-held areas.

Responding to the criticism, Mengistu implemented an austerity program in February 1985 aimed at saving the famine victims. The program called for all Ethiopians to donate part of their salaries to relief efforts, asked citizens to serve in shelters and rehabilitation camps, and offered policies designed to conserve water and soil.

Experts believe that unless modern farming technology is

introduced immediately, the nation will become a barren desert unable to feed itself.

Ethiopian Jews,

sometimes referred to as "black Jews," are believed to be descendants of the tribe of Dan, one of the original tribes of Israel.

In 1977, there were an estimated twenty-five thousand Ethiopian Jews, most of them living in the northern provinces ravaged by drought and famine. Ethiopians call the Jews "Falashas," a derogatory term meaning "strangers," and for centuries the Falashas have been subject to religious persecution.

According to the Israeli Law of Return, any Jew coming to Israel is eligible for immediate friendship. Since 1977, Israel has been helping Ethiopian Jews escape the persecution and famine of Ethiopia. An airlift called "Operation Moses" has brought an estimated fifteen thousand Ethiopian Jews to Israel. The relocation effort was a closely guarded secret—until early 1985 when an Israeli immigration official bragged about its effectiveness at a cocktail party in London.

Upon learning of the airlift, most of the world applauded Israel's humanitarianism. Even countries violently opposed to Israel's policies commended the apparent dedication to religious principles behind the airlift.

Ethiopian officials complained that Israel was interfering with its internal affairs and called the airlift "sinister." After the airlift was halted, Israel's Prime Minister Shimon Peres vowed to continue rescue efforts, "We shall not rest until our brothers and sisters from Ethiopia are safely home," Peres said.

Exclusionary Rule

is a judicial ruling stating that no evidence gathered by police through violations of a suspect's constitutional rights is admissable at trial and must therefore be "excluded."

During 1984, the Supreme Court established two exceptions to the rule. The first, which is now known as "the inevitable discovery" exception, grew out of a case in which a confession obtained improperly led police to the body of a murder victim.

The defendant's attorneys argued that since evidence (the body) was obtained illegally (through the confession), it should have been excluded. Prosecutors pointed out that a massive search for the victim's body was underway before the confession was obtained, and since the body wasn't very well hidden, it would have been found anyway.

The court ruled that if it can be proven that illegally obtained evidence would have surfaced "inevitably," that evidence is admissible.

The second exception, called the "good faith" exception, has generated considerable controversy. The exception grew out of a case in which a magistrate had filled out the wrong forms to grant a warrant that the police requested. The warrant allowed the police to seize evidence that finally led to a criminal conviction.

The defense in this case tried to have the evidence thrown out of court, claiming that it had been gathered through the use of an illegal warrant. The court, however, upheld the defendant's conviction on the grounds that the police had acted "in good faith" to secure a valid search warrant.

Critics of the ruling warned that the "good faith" exception could easily lead police forces to place expediency before rights guaranteed by the Constitution.

Expert Witnesses

are established authorities in a variety of disciplines, including medicine, engineering, biology, handwriting, and behavioral sciences among others. Their testimony in court proceedings—and in nonjudicial hearings—is often used to help resolve complicated issues involving lives or millions of dollars. Their role in the litigation process is expanding as our society becomes more technically and scientifically oriented.

An industry of sorts has emerged to coordinate the services of expert witnesses. Expert Witness Network, a Washington, D.C., firm, uses computers to match specialists with cases requiring their expertise. A publication called the *Forensics Services Directory* lists hundreds of experts, available (for a fee) in specialties such as adhesives, auto accidents, pediatric malpractice, libel/slander, product liability, the stock market, and toxic chemicals. The expert witness "industry" held its first convention in 1984.

Although variable by specialty, expertise has a strong market value. Trial preparation fees run from $20 to $250 an hour. Testimony can cost more than $2,000 per day. Experts resent the occasional accusations that their testimony is influenced by their "hired gun" status. Ethical standards adhered to by most experts require strict objectivity and prohibit the acceptance of fees contingent on the outcome of a case. Cynics point out, however, that if an expert receives frequent assignments from, say, an insurance company, it's doubtful the expert's testimony will ever *hurt* the company's cases.

Increasingly, experts are being used as mediators in non-judicial disputes, especially in highly technical conflicts where they are more useful as arbitrators than are judges.

"We are moving toward an era of scientific judgment," said Professor Oliver Schroeder of Case Western University late in 1984.

Farm Crisis

is a phrase often used to describe bleak economic conditions in the U.S. agriculture industry.

Since 1981, more than twenty thousand U.S. farms have

been auctioned off. Thousands of farmers have given up their land, selling out to agricultural combines and conglomerates. An estimated one-third of U.S. farmers have serious financial problems and 10 percent are on the edge of financial disaster. More than 30 percent of government-insured farm loans ($8 billion) are delinquent.

The crisis had its beginnings in the 1970s when the Soviet Union began buying huge amounts of U.S. grain, and predictions of global famine caused thousands of Americans to return to the farm. Farmers already in business expanded their operations and seventy thousand new farmers appeared. All borrowed heavily (with government encouragement and assistance in many cases). Farm land escalated in price from $300 an acre to $800.

Global recession, high interest rates, a rise in the value of the dollar, and a series of political embargoes all contributed to burst the farm-boom bubble in the early 1980s. Farm income began to fall sharply, and farmers found themselves owing more on loan interest than they got for their crops.

The crisis seems to have hit hardest the so-called "family farm": medium sized operations of three to five hundred acres which are too small to run efficiently without sophisticated equipment and too big to allow the farmer to take a supplemental job.

Some observers claim that there is no farm crisis, simply a natural "shakeout" dictated by the marketplace. If the family farm can't survive, so be it, they say. It's because they can't operate with what the market wants to pay them for their goods. If not for extravagant government farm policy these family farms would have disappeared long ago, the argument concludes.

Farmers disagree, contending that high interest rates and the artificially strong dollar (both conditions related to the federal deficit) are beyond their control. If they are forced out of business, farmers believe the conglomerates left in farming will eliminate competition—and that will lead, ultimately, to higher food prices.

Federal Deficit

is the amount by which government expenditures exceed government revenues. The deficit can be reduced by higher taxes, lower spending levels, or some combination thereof.

The federal budget has been balanced only once since 1959, and recently, government spending has been approaching the astronomical stage, headed for one trillion dollars per year. (Spending a million dollars a day, it would take almost three thousand years to spend a trillion dollars.)

Soon, almost one-quarter of the total U.S. economic output will have to be spent to cover the interest on the national debt (previous deficits which the government had to borrow to make up).

Political considerations make tax increases and spending reductions needed to cut the deficit difficult to implement. President Reagan has adamantly refused to consider a tax increase, contending that economic growth will generate higher tax revenues and lower the need for expenditures on food stamps, unemployment compensation, and other welfare programs. Growth, coupled with domestic spending cuts will bring the deficit under control, the Reagan administration claims.

About 30 percent of the federal budget pays for defense. Another 20 percent goes for Social Security, and about 15 percent of the budget is needed to pay interest on previous deficits. Since Reagan has declared defense and Social Security off limits and because the interest on previous debts must be paid, the question occurs: What's to cut?

Social programs, the administration has declared, must be slashed drastically. Not enough, say opponents, and unfair besides. Also, how does government, made up of politicians, deal with the wrath of special-interest groups affected by such cuts? Veterans, retirees, teachers, businesses, and a host of other special interests will fight cuts vigorously.

Many legislators support across-the-board cuts or a general spending freeze to reduce the deficit. Some projections indicate that, at current economic growth rates, the budget could be balanced within five to six years if a freeze (or modest cuts) were implemented immediately.

Other deficit-reduction proposals suggest increasing revenue through elimination of tax deductions, credits, and shelters.

The huge federal deficit alarms economists because of its effect on so many other aspects of the economy. Because the government needs to borrow so much, interest rates remain high, and the increased borrowing fuels bigger deficits in the future.

The high interest rates caused by federal borrowing attracts foreign investors and keeps the dollar artificially inflated. The high value of the dollar makes U.S. exports expensive and imports cheap, costing American jobs. Because federal borrowing absorbs about half of available credit in the economy, it drains funds from the economy that could be used for industrial expansion and modernization, which would ordinarily generate growth and jobs. Housing construction funds are also affected. In short, the deficit saps economic strength, and, if unchecked, could lead to a serious recession.

Federal Housing Administration (FHA)

is a U.S. government agency created in 1934 to insure home mortgages and to stimulate the American housing industry at a time when almost no new homes were being built. The FHA provides guarantees which secure housing loans made by private banks and other approved lenders. FHA guarantees allow lenders to offer mortgages at interest rates slightly below the prevailing market rate.

Because houses purchased with FHA-backed mortgages must meet certain construction standards, the agency has had a major effect on the quality of housing in the United States.

In 1965, the FHA became a part of the Department of

Housing and Urban Development (HUD). Previously, FHA mortgages were available only for single-family homes. The agency may now issue loans for multifamily dwellings and public housing projects. (*See* HUD)

Federal Reserve System,

often referred to as the "the Fed," is the nation's central bank and acts as the federal government's basic tool for creating money and regulating the amount of money and credit in the U.S. economy.

Established by Congress in 1913, the Fed is not an agency of the U.S. government. Rather, it is a national "superbank" owned by its member banks. The members include all nationally chartered banks, plus most state-chartered banks, so that banks belonging to the system hold about 85 percent of all deposits in the country.

Despite private ownership, however, the Fed is intimately linked to the U.S. government. The president of the United States appoints the seven people who make up the Fed's Board of Governors, and that primary board, in turn, appoints board members who supervise each of the Fed's twelve district banks.

Together, the Fed and its district banks work to increase or decrease the nation's money supply in order to balance a series of conflicting national needs, such as maintaining high employment but keeping wages reasonable; maintaining high factory output while controlling prices; and creating sufficient credit for business expansion and building construction without setting off inflation (*see* Inflation).

When the Fed increases the money supply it is said to be following a policy of "easy money"; when it restricts credit and the creation of new money the bank is said to be following a policy of "tight money."

The Federal Open Market Committee—the Board of Governors and presidents of five of the district banks—meets every three weeks to decide whether it will ease or tighten the supply of money issued by the district banks to their members and, hence, to the economy as a whole.

To tighten the money supply, a Federal Reserve bank sells government securities through a network of dealers, who in turn sell them to commercial banks. In paying for the securities, the banks remove money from the economy (causing interest rates to rise).

To loosen the money supply, the Fed buys securities, paying for them with checks it draws on itself. These checks increase the supplies of money that member banks lend to their customers (making loans more affordable).

Over the long haul the Fed has tended to ease the money supply in order to promote expansion of the economy and accommodate population growth. If used indiscriminately, however, easy money can lead to inflation. In response to a series of severe inflationary outbreaks in the 1970s, President Jimmy Carter in 1979 appointed Paul Volcker as chairman of the Fed. Volcker, well known for his tough approach to monetary policy, instituted a tight-money policy that succeeded in controlling inflation but also brought on an economic recession in 1981–82. The recession, the worst since the Great Depression of the 1930s, subjected Volcker and the Fed to sharp criticism from the business community and many government figures.

Federal Trade Commission (FTC)

was created in 1914 to prevent unfair competition in the American business system. The agency has the power to investigate business practices, issue complaints, and enforce cease-and-desist orders.

Composed of five members appointed to seven-year terms by the President, the FTC's primary concern is the enforcement of antitrust legislation which forbids monopolies and price-fixing. The FTC is also authorized to prosecute in cases of false advertising.

Recently, the FTC instituted trade practice conferences,

in which industry representatives assist FTC officials in formulating fair trade practice rules which (after hearings) become federal regulations carrying the force of law.

Feminism

is a movement aimed at achieving status and rights for women equal to those of men. Several national and numerous local organizations call themselves feminist, as do millions of unaffiliated women and men. (The term "women's liberation" is rarely used anymore.)

The philosophical goal of feminism is to change society so that the relationship of men and women will change to one of equality. Feminists strive to eradicate patriarchy (a father's control of family life) and sexism (conscious or subconscious beliefs that women are sex toys) or discrimination because of gender. Feminism's practical goals include ending job and pay discriminations, establishing a system of tax-supported daycare centers, and gaining equal treatment under state and federal laws.

Although the origins of feminism go back to the nineteenth century women's suffrage movement, it wasn't until the 1960s that any appreciable effect on society was noticed. Feminists of twenty years ago used the tools of radical protests to make their presence felt: marches, invasion of male sanctuaries, and condemnation of female sex symbols.

Because women constitute a majority of voting age Americans, feminism is no longer considered radical, and it is fast becoming an integral part of contemporary society.

Federal Investigative Strike Team (FIST)

is a nationwide program in which federal, state, and local law-enforcement forces work together to track down and capture fugitives who have been on the run for months, or sometimes years.

In an eight-week campaign ending in November 1984, FIST operations resulted in the capture of 3,309 fugitives wanted in eight eastern states. The fugitives were implicated in more than twelve thousand felonies, with thirty-four facing murder charges. Former Attorney General William French Smith called the roundup "the most successful fugitive manhunt in law enforcement history."

FIST's targets were career criminals. Some escaped from prison, others fled after being found guilty of felonies, still others were avoiding arrest. According to the federal marshals who organized and supervised FIST manhunts, local police are usually too busy with new crime to devote much manpower to finding fugitives from old cases.

Although a handful of suspects have been easily found (hanging around old haunts), most FIST operations are laborious and often dangerous. Officers have developed several successful "stings" to lure their quarry out of hiding, sending word that fugitives have packages waiting at a bogus delivery service, or promising job interviews.

FIST operations are expensive, costing an average $8,000 for each fugitive apprehended, but strike-team members insist it is money well spent. In discussing one habitual offender captured by FIST, federal marshal Dave O'Flaherty said: "If we can get him off the street for a week or a month, that may be one murder or robbery he won't be able to commit."

Flat-Rate Income Tax

is a taxing approach that would eliminate most deductions and impose one (flat) tax rate on all income brackets.

Experts agree that a pure flat-rate tax has no chance of becoming law, but, at the end of 1984, considerable congressional support could be found for modified flat-rate proposals. In the modified approach, taxpayers would be allowed to keep certain "sacred cow" exemptions—mortgage interest (residence only), charitable contributions, IRAs, local and state taxes, and heavy medical expenses. The fifteen tax rates currently in effect (ranging from 11 to 50 percent) would be reduced to two or three (ranging from 14 to 35 percent).

Proponents of the modified flat-rate system claim that the approach has several advantages. People with equal income would pay the same tax, distributing the overall tax burden more fairly than it is distributed now. Eliminating complex deductions and credits would make taxes easier to calculate and enforce, and banish the dubious tax shelters now used, freeing capital for productive investment.

Flat taxers predict that, under the structure they advocate, 70 percent of the population would pay the same or lower taxes than they do now. The 30 percent who would pay more include those now taking full advantage of deductions, loopholes, and tax shelters. Businesses would pay more also. Although flat-tax plans reduce the top corporate income tax rate from 46 to 33 percent, most business writeoffs would be eliminated.

The flat-rate approach is popular with many congressmen and senators, and has public support, but attempts to reduce the federal deficit may delay serious discussion of the proposal until 1986 or 1987. (See Federal Deficit)

Food and Drug Administration (FDA)

is a federal agency that oversees the safety of all foods, drugs, cosmetics, and medical devices (such as pacemakers and artificial limbs) sold in the United States.

Although most of the publicity the FDA attracts is generated by its evaluations of drugs and medicines, a sizeable portion (more than a third) of the agency's budget is used to ensure the purity of food. The FDA was established in 1906 in response to widespread complaints about untested additives in processed foods.

The manufacturers of drugs and medicines seeking FDA approval of their products must submit to rigorous testing procedures. In addition to its own testing, the FDA solicits the opinions of outside medical experts. Drugs must be proven safe *and* effective before FDA approval is granted.

Pharmaceutical companies and physicians occasionally have accused the FDA of being too slow and too strict in its approval procedure. In response to this kind of criticism, the FDA in 1982 set up a "fast track" process to review exceptionally promising new drugs.

The FDA found it necessary to assume regulation of medical devices when certain pacemakers began malfunctioning, and when the Dalkon Shield, an intrauterine birth-control device, killed several women and left others sterile.

Food Stamps

were designed to improve nutrition in low income households. Administered by the U.S. Department of Agriculture through state and local agencies, the food stamp program tries to assure that no one suffers from hunger because of a temporary —or permanent—decline in income.

Surveys indicate that the general public approves of the food stamp program, despite its frequent abuse.

Forensics

is an expanding professional field that uses several branches of science to solve criminal cases. Forensic specialists play a vital role in criminal trials, where they often testify as expert witnesses. (*See* Expert Witnesses)

Several areas of scientific knowledge come into play in modern criminology. A pathologist determines the cause of sudden or unexpected death. A toxicologist isolates poisons found in a victim's body. A forensic anthropologist identifies decomposed parts and skeletal remains. A forensic odontologist analyzes dental records to identify remains, and matches teeth with bite marks found on a body. Other forensic specialists study physical evidence to establish a link between victim and suspect. Hair, fibers, soil, blood, paint chips, firearms, fingerprints, handwriting, voice prints, and even skin cells are examined meticulously.

Forensic specialists work in crime laboratories. There are about three hundred such labs run by local, state, and federal police agencies. The world's largest crime lab is operated by the U.S. Federal Bureau of Investigation (FBI).

A Fortune of Admiration

IBM, International Business Machines, is the most admired U.S. corporation according to *Fortune* magazine.

Fortune's annual survey evaluates the reputation of two hundred and fifty companies in twenty-five of the country's largest industries. A poll of eight thousand executives, directors, and financial analysts was used to rate companies in several areas: quality of management, quality of products or services, innovation, investment value, financial stability, the ability to attract and keep talented employees, community and environmental responsibility, and use of assets. IBM did well in all categories, with one notable exception—innovation.

The least admired U.S. firm in 1984 was Continental Illinois Corporation, whose Chicago bank (one of the nation's largest) had to be bailed out by the federal government.

American Motors Corporation, one of the survey's ten least admired companies, reacted bitterly to its ranking. "If *Fortune* magazine was admired more than it is, it might affect us," said an AMC vice-president. "I think it is more scientific to exchange valentines in kindergarten than the way they conduct the survey."

Freedom of Information Act

is a law enacted in 1966 that requires federal agencies to allow citizen-access to public records.

The Freedom of Information Act is regarded by legal and political authorities as an important vehicle through which government officials can be held accountable for their actions. By invoking this law, citizens have found their names on FBI and CIA surveillance lists and have sometimes discovered dossiers filled with hearsay evidence and rumor.

The law does, however, permit certain exceptions: government disclosures (including confidential personnel files, national defense data, law enforcement records, and financial records), materials related to weapons systems, and financial data which, if disclosed, would have allowed private individuals to reap huge profits in the stock market.

But when a government agency withholds information on the basis of one of the allowable exemptions, the law allows citizens to sue for disclosure. A court can then decide if the information sought can legally be withheld.

Full-Court Press,

in basketball is end-to-end pressure; a defensive strategy designed to create offense by shadowing opponents all over the floor. In government, a full-court press is a feverish, relentless effort by administrative officials, lobbyists, and other supporters to have proposed legislation passed. In either case, the full-court press gives the "pressed" little time to think or plan.

Gender Gap

was the phrase used to characterize the supposed differences in social outlook and electoral preferences between men and women in the 1984 election. Results of that election proved that the gap was almost indiscernible.

General Dynamics

is the U.S. Department of Defense's largest supplier of military hardware.

One of America's first conglomerates (see Conglomerate), General Dynamics was founded in 1952. Its 1984 sales of $7.8 billion earned the corporation a profit of about $382 million.

Early in 1985, Defense Secretary Casper Weinberger suspended Pentagon payments to the corporation, pending investigation of its billing practices.

During the investigation, it was learned that one of General Dynamics' directors had been involved in a scheme to bribe legislators. Congressional reaction to this revelation included branding the director as "a crook" and a demand that his security clearance be rescinded.

Further embarrassment for General Dynamics was generated by the discovery that the firm had billed the United States for a $100,000 corporate meeting held at a Charleston, S.C., resort. Included in these expenses were some $1,100 earrings, a $155 charge for kennel fees incurred by a dog belonging to a General Dynamics official, and several $350-per-night hotel rooms.

Because the U.S. government is the source of about 90 percent of General Dynamics' revenue, the firm would be in serious trouble should the Pentagon abandon its products.

Prior to its difficulties, General Dynamics had an impressive history. Working with Admiral Hyman Rickover, "Father of the nuclear navy," the corporation produced a fleet of nuclear submarines, starting with the Nautilus, considered a milestone in naval history.

General Dynamics also built the first Atlas ICBM; the first rocket used in the Mercury astronaut program; and the Voyager 2, now approaching Uranus and on its way to Neptune. The company currently builds equipment for all branches of the U.S. armed forces (including fighters, missiles, ships, and tanks).

Genetic Engineering

is the breeding and manipulation of living cells to produce drugs, hormones, enzymes, and other organisms. Some scientists believe that genetic engineering is on the verge of revolutionizing the way we live.

Applications of genetic engineering well along in the research stage include producing hormones that will correct growth disorders in children and help treat burns, fractures, and diseases of the elderly, and enzymes that transform solid waste into useful sugars and alcohol. (An enzyme that eats oil spills has been available for some time.)

Genetically engineered insulin is already on the market. Vaccines for hepatitis, malaria, rabies, and venereal disease are being tested.

Many investment analysts believe that genetic engineering will reestablish the United States as the world's leader in technology and manufacturing.

There are obvious hazards in expanding this relatively new science. New diseases could conceivably be created, or human cells altered in such a way that the basic characteristics of future generations are radically modified.

Genetic engineering has already aroused opposition among environmentalists, and the Humane Society.

In April 1984, environmental activist Jeremy Rifkin sued to stop experiments in which genetically altered organisms were to be released in farm fields. Researchers at the University of California had planned to spray potato fields with bacteria that could prevent the crop from freezing. Rifkin charged that the bacteria might reach the upper atmosphere, block ice formation there, and reduce precipitation over wide areas. Scientists dismissed that fear, but agreed that a thorough evaluation of environmental effects should be mandatory prior to the release of new organisms.

In October, Rifkin joined with the Humane Society to try to stop gene-transfer experiments involving pig and sheep embryos. Researchers would like to improve livestock breeding by introducing genes that stimulate growth, or make animals less vulnerable to disease. Rifkin charged that these kinds of experiments are cruel to animals, and violate an animal's "right to exist as a separate, identifiable creature."

Genetic engineers view this sort of opposition as nonsensical and ill-informed. Inherited diseases (such as hemophilia and sickle-cell anemia), they point out, could be treated by replacing missing or defective genes with healthy ones. Important cures, they say, will be possible only if gene-transfer experiments are allowed to continue.

Gentrification

is a term used to describe the transformation undergone by an urban neighborhood "reclaimed" by affluent professionals.

Typically, gentrification takes hold after several old, shaky buildings in a neighborhood have been rehabilitated ("rehabbed") and sold for nice prices to young professionals who like the nostalgic charm and the location (usually near the heart of the city). Property values rise as the rehabilitation effort spreads through the immediate areas. Laundromats, shoe repair and "mom and pop" shops close. Boutiques and health food stores open. Bars decorated with hanging plants and wicker replace neighborhood bars.

For those who own property in the neighborhood, gentrification is wonderful. For low-income residents forced to move because they can no longer afford the rent, it is a curse.

Recent demonstrations in Chicago and San Francisco have protested the economics of gentrification and the loss of affordable housing.

Good Samaritan Laws

formalize the principle that any person who helps another in obvious distress or danger cannot be held liable for any harm inadvertently caused by that assistance.

The laws, which don't apply in cases where malice or gross negligence can be proven, were enacted primarily to protect doctors, forced to practice emergency street medicine, from malpractice suits.

Governor Gloom

is the media nickname given to Colorado's chief executive Richard D. Lamm, because of his insistence that the American public needs to accept and deal with some harsh economic truths: for instance, that Social Security, Medicare, and similar programs will eventually bankrupt the United States if they are not changed.

Lamm first attracted national attention in 1984 when he commented that the terminally ill have a "duty to die and get out of the way . . . and let the other society, our kids, build a reasonable life." He is also quick to remind his constituents that government cannot ensure the happiness and health of each citizen and that the "welfare state" conception of government must end if the country is to remain solvent. "This nation is in deep trouble, trouble deeper than most people recognize. I find a need to say that," said Lamm in a recent interview.

In 1986 Lamm, a Democrat, will finish his third term as governor of Colorado. He claims he has no plans to seek reelection or to run for Senator Gary Hart's Senate seat, should Hart again decide to run for the presidency. Lamm said he viewed "six years in Washington not to be a term, but a sentence."

Green Movement,

considered to be a new direction in political thinking, has coalesced into an ecology party, which has done well in recent French and West German elections. Members of the Green Movement believe that a realistic ecological perspective must be incorporated into all political and economic policy.

Advocates of Green Movement doctrine argue that economic growth and technological advances can't continue forever. Eventually, they say, the world will run out of raw materials and sources of nonrenewable energy.

The Green Movement wants to stabilize the need for the earth's resources, and minimize human impact on the environment. Its members are trying to redefine national goals in terms of ecology and basic human needs.

Grenada

is a small Caribbean island nation that the United States invaded in 1983.

About the size of Detroit, Grenada has a population of 110,000. The island, discovered by Christopher Columbus in 1498, was a British possession until 1974, when an independent government headed by Eric Gairy was established. In 1979, the New Jewel Movement, led by Castro protégé Maurice Bishop, seized power. Bishop adopted some leftist policies, but he did not move quickly or forcefully enough to suit the more militant Marxists in his party. In October 1983, an extremist group took over the government and Bishop was murdered.

Shortly thereafter, convinced that Cuba was using Grenada to build a military base, the United States and several Caribbean allies invaded the island to help "restore democracy" and to "rescue" 250 American medical students that the Reagan administration said were in danger. U.S. forces met resistance from Cuban troops and found a partially completed airfield and several cases of weapons.

In December 1984, Grenada held an election won by the moderate New National party. The United States promised $25 million in aid and a new mental hospital to replace the one destroyed by U.S. bombs in the 1983 invasion. The Reagan administration hoped that the election of a friendly regime would help increase U.S. investments in Grenada. At the end of 1984, 250 American troops were stationed on the island. New prime minister Herbert Blaize has asked them to stay.

Greying of America

For the first time in history, there are more Americans over age sixty-five than there are teenagers. As the number of older people increases, the strain on the Social Security and Medicare (already near the breaking point) becomes enormous. No solutions to these expensive problems seem imminent. This aging (greying) of the United States is raising problems the nation has never faced before and has no experience in solving.

The average American man's life expectancy is seventy-nine and one-half years. Women, on the average, can expect to live about five years longer.

According to sociologist Aaron Lipman of the University of Miami, the question of how to care for the elderly requires a concentrated national effort. "The problem," Lipman said, "is how much to apportion to private industry, how much to government, how much to volunteerism?"

Lipman believes that American commercialism will provide some assistance. "When money can be made from it, someone will try to satisfy the needs of the elderly. It has begun already, with leisure cities, apartment sizes smaller and more convenient to maintain, food packaged for one, and the tremendous growth of travel tours for the elderly."

Gross National Product (GNP)

is the monetary value of all goods and services produced by a nation's economy during a year.

The GNP of the United States in 1984 was calculated by the U.S. Department of Commerce as $3.764 trillion. This was 6.9 percent above the 1983 GNP and represented the strongest annual growth in the nation's economy since 1951, when a rise of 8.3 percent occurred.

About two-thirds of the U.S. GNP consists of money spent by consumers for goods and services. Government spending (purchases by 81,000 units of federal, state, county, and municipal government) accounts for almost one-quarter of the GNP.

The GNP is an important figure because it reflects an economy's ability to produce wealth. Year-to-year changes in the GNP indicate whether the economy is growing fast enough to produce jobs and business opportunities for all who need them, and whether it is generating wealth at a sufficient rate for individuals to improve their standard of living.

Guatemala,

once the site of an ancient Mayan Indian civilization, is the farthest north of the Central American nations, and one of the countries which President Reagan claims is in danger from Nicaragua. (See Nicaragua)

Guatemala, the training and debarkation site for the disastrous Bay of Pigs invasion launched by Cuban refugees with CIA assistance in 1961, has been ruled by military force for most of its national life, although a legitimate democracy has occasionally emerged.

During the 1970s, Guatemala experienced waves of political violence from the left and the right (*see* Political Spectrum), until General José Ríos Montt declared a state of seige and pursued a war effort designed to exterminate left-wing guerrillas. The massacres resulting from that effort caused the Carter administration to cut off U.S. aid to Guatemala.

General Oscar Mejía Victores seized power in 1983 and, surprisingly, the elections he promised occurred in July 1984. Moderates won leadership positions in the new government and, for the moment, Guatemala is once again a democracy. President Reagan has requested that military and economic aid to Guatemala be resumed.

Gunboat Diplomacy,

a phrase usually used derogatorily, describes diplomatic relations conducted in the shadow of threatened force: negotiations at the embassy, gunboats in the harbor.

President Reagan has been accused of gunboat diplomacy in his administration's relations with several Latin American countries.

Guerrilla,

meaning "little war" in Spanish, was first used to describe bands of Spanish irregulars who raided, harassed, and sabotaged Napoleon's army, disappearing after each attack into inaccessible mountain strongholds. The word is now used to describe unconventional soldiers and the movements to which they belong.

Guerrillas avoid open warfare and rely on surprise ambushes and acts of terrorism—an effective strategy in certain terrains, as the Viet Cong proved in Vietnam. During World War II, poorly armed, half-starved Yugoslavian guerrillas took advantage of natural strongholds to pin down as many as ten German divisions at a time.

Some cities in unstable nations are infested with "urban guerrillas" who hide in slums and venture out to bomb banks or kidnap foreign businessmen.

Hackers

are usually teenagers whose world revolves around computers. Using their own personal computers and inexpensive attachments that make automated phone calls, hackers spend most of their free time trying to exploit and conquer computer technology.

Using their computers to locate access numbers for long-distance services, for example, hackers have placed "free" calls worth hundreds of thousands of dollars ($140,000 in one instance).

A hacker gains access to someone else's computer by programming his own processor to dial hundreds of telephone numbers. When his phone receives a computer tone, the hacker is "in" the system. This practice is called "phone phreaking."

Because most companies construct their computer systems to be "user friendly" (capable of being used by new employees with only a few days' training), hackers find that getting into an industrial system is not that difficult. The hacker simply types in HELP, TEST, SYSTEM, or some other simple command and the computer tells him whatever he needs to know to penetrate further. Hackers have broken into systems belonging to schools, mortgage companies, airlines, hospitals, credit bureaus, and have even stumbled into secret Pentagon systems.

Hackers communicate with each other via electronic bulletin boards (access files where they can leave and retrieve messages). There are hundreds of thousands of bulletin boards, many of which are monitored for leads by police departments and other security forces.

According to computer experts, most hackers are not unusually intelligent; they just have unlimited time to pursue their particular quest. Authorities acknowledge that hackers are expensive nuisances, difficult to catch if they get in and out of systems once or twice, but easier to find if they keep raiding one particular computer.

Hackers who access commercial or government systems are considered criminals, even when their crimes are restricted to electronic trespassing.

Headhunters

are employment agencies which specialize in finding jobs for top executives and executives for top jobs. Salaries of headhunters' clients typically reach the six-figure range, of which headhunters take a third as a one-time commission.

Heavy Metal

is hard, harsh rock-and-roll which relies on hyperamplified electric guitars. Vocals are elementary, delivered in a hoarse scream.

A crude, powerful steel girder of sound, heavy metal is also known as "sledge rock" and "crunch rock." The belligerent music, played at ear-popping decibel levels, is the stock in trade of such groups as Twisted Sister, Ratt, AC/DC, Iron

Maiden, and Judas Priest. Heavy metal stage shows typically are violent affairs featuring explosions and the wreckage of instruments. The musicians present bizarre, sometimes brutal images, often dressing in chains and leather. Heavy metal appeals primarily to teenage boys and has been associated with violence.

High Tech

is an abbreviation of high technology, a phrase used to refer to the products of what some historians call the Second Industrial Revolution. Television, computers, robots, and other electronic wonders are all high-tech products.

The phrase is also used to describe new styles of architecture, interior decorating, furniture, lighting—anything looking "post-industrial."

Home Rule

powers grant to city or county governments a degree of autonomy usually coupled with the power to tax. Proponents of home rule say it provides a government that is "closest to the people." Opponents contend that many localities lack the political will to institute unpopular but necessary taxes.

Honduras,

a Central American nation which borders both El Salvador and Nicaragua, hosts a strong U.S. military presence and is considered the major base for American forces in the region.

In 1969, a border dispute between Honduras and El Salvador left a thousand dead and tens of thousands homeless. A series of military dictators who ruled Honduras between 1972 and 1982 left the nation's economy in shambles. In 1982, a parliamentary democracy was installed with Roberto Suazo Córdova's election as the Honduran president.

During 1984, Honduras received $125 million in U.S. military and economic aid—assistance not gratefully accepted by all Hondurans. Several officials asked the United States to de-emphasize military ties and help establish a stable political and economic system.

About twelve thousand Nicaraguan contras (see Contras) use Honduras as a base from which to fight the Sandinist government. The United States trains Honduran and Salvadoran troops at Honduran installations.

In 1984, the United States and its Central American allies staged extensive training exercises in Honduras. A Pentagon spokesperson said that the maneuvers were held to remind Nicaragua that "perhaps it shouldn't have designs on its neighbors."

Hospital Heroin

is prescribed by reputable physicians and administered in hospitals to relieve the pain of terminal cancer victims. Early in 1985, a bill introduced into the U.S. Senate asked Congress to allow physicians to prescribe the drug. The bill is co-sponsored by liberals, conservatives, and moderates of both parties.

When a similar proposal reached the House of Representatives several years ago, it was soundly defeated; congressmen feared that hospital heroin would increase hospital robberies. Others suggested that the heroin would be diverted to street sales.

Proponents of hospital heroin point out that about eight thousand Americans die each year in agony and that the administration of heroin can help substantially to reduce that pain: it is faster-acting than morphine, twice as potent, and has fewer side effects. England and other nations already make heroin available to terminal cancer victims.

The bill's supporters also point out that only 2 percent of drug-related robberies occur in hospitals, and that only fifteen pounds of the drug a year would be needed to implement the program on a nationwide basis. An affirmative vote, they conclude, is no evidence that the Senate is "going soft on drugs."

Housing and Urban Development (HUD)

is a cabinet-level agency created in 1965 to improve the quality of housing, particularly in the nation's metropolitan areas. HUD's programs include mortgage assistance and rent subsidies for low-income groups, and urban renewal and development projects undertaken in partnership with local housing authorities. The department's Urban Development Action Grant program attempts to generate private investment in economically depressed areas by providing "seed money" to develop industrial parks, shopping centers, and apartment complexes.

Until 1982, most of HUD's budget was devoted to the construction and maintenance of low- to moderate-income housing. The department's efforts to build this housing in middle-class neighborhoods invariably sparked protest and resentment among residents. These protests frequently had racial undertones.

Under President Reagan's administration, HUD has shifted its efforts toward the rehabilitation of existing housing. The department is also trying to obtain congressional authorization for Urban Enterprise Zones (see Urban Enterprise Zones)—designated city neighborhoods where new businesses could receive substantial tax relief.

Human Rights

are basic individual freedoms which no moral government should restrict or revoke. They include freedom of speech, the right to vote in free elections, freedom of religion, the right to privacy, freedom to petition the government to resolve a grievance, the right to peaceable assembly, and freedom of the press.

All the rights cited above are guaranteed to U.S. citizens by the Constitution, yet in many nations they do not exist. The United States has adopted a policy of promoting and protecting human rights on a worldwide basis.

Former President Jimmy Carter tried to establish a consistent human rights stance, criticizing totalitarian governments not only in Communist countries, but also among U.S. allies such as the Philippines, South Korea, and Chile. Carter reduced or halted economic aid to several repressive regimes, winning the reinstatement of several political prisoners.

But Carter's policy had glaring exceptions. Because the United States needed oil and a strong Mideast ally, Carter's administration (as had Nixon's) backed the Shah of Iran with extensive military aid—despite the fifty thousand political opponents the Shah had jailed or killed.

The Reagan administration has tended to pursue what he often describes as a "pragmatic" approach to the human rights issue, minimizing the importance of violations committed by U.S. allies, but critizing repression in the Soviet Union and in its satellite countries and allies.

Hypermarket

is the word coined to describe Bigg's supermarket in Cincinnati, Ohio. Appropriately named, Bigg's has forty checkout lanes and seventy-five aisles 150 yards long (almost the length of a city block). The store stocks sixty thousand items, four times as many as a traditional supermarket—everything from cantaloupes to car parts, fettucine to floppy disks, TV dinners to televisions to eat them in front of.

"We're neither a supermarket nor a department store. We're both," said Jacques Le Foll, vice-president of the company that owns Bigg's (Hyper Shoppers, Inc.). Le Foll sees the experimental store as a prototype for others. "We hope to open five each year across the country," Le Foll said.

The hypermarket philosophy is based on extremely high volume, lower prices than the competition's, and minimal overhead. Fixtures and decor at Bigg's represent the bare minimum needed to keep the store from looking like an airplane hangar.

Since opening in October 1984, Bigg's has attracted more than fifty thousand shoppers a week—five times the traffic of a typical supermarket. Its annual sales are expected to exceed $100 million. There have been problems, however. Despite all those checkout lanes, Saturday morning lines are often an hour long.

Ibuprofen

is a nonprescription pain reliever. Marketed under the brand names Advil and Nuprin, ibuprofen is especially effective in the treatment of menstrual cramps. The drug provides 80–95 percent relief (compared with 30 percent averaged by aspirin).

Less likely to cause stomach irritation than aspirin, ibuprofen relieves pain by blocking the production of prostaglandins—the substances produced by the body that regulate pain, inflammation, and fever. In addition to menstrual cramps, ibuprofen is effective against other pain, especially dental irritation.

Before being approved for over-the-counter sale, ibuprofen was the drug most often prescribed for arthritis patients. Concern about the drug's safety centers on the risk of kidney damage in diabetics and the elderly. Ibuprofen may also prove dangerous to those who suffer from high-blood pressure or take diuretics for premenstrual tension.

Late in 1984, the National Kidney Foundation called for strongly worded, detailed warning on ibuprofen labels. Better yet, the foundation suggested, druggists should keep ibuprofen behind the counter, selling it only after carefully counseling customers.

Ideology

originally meant a system of ideas and theories for political and social conduct. Now it is a word used disdainfully to imply blind rigidity or narrow-mindedness. Ideology has come to mean the opposite of rationality and pragmatism.

Indictment

is a formal, written accusation issued after a grand jury has determined that there is sufficient evidence to charge a suspect with criminal activity. The indictment also serves to inform the accused of the charges against him and, by law, must do so clearly enough to enable the defendant to prepare a defense.

Perhaps because the differences between a grand jury and a trial jury are not clear, the public often associates a grand jury indictment with guilt. An indictment may thus destroy the career of a public figure, even if the accusations are never proven at trial.

Individual Retirement Account (IRA)

is a personal, tax-sheltered retirement plan. It was developed to provide all American workers with an opportunity to build a more secure financial future.

An individual wage earner may contribute up to $2,000 a year to an IRA. If the wage earner's spouse is also employed, he or she can establish a separate IRA and also contribute up to $2,000 annually.

All IRA contributions are tax deductible, a direct reduction of gross income. The deduction is available even to those who do not itemize. The interest income earned by an IRA does not become taxable until the wage earner begins withdrawing from the IRA.

What's the catch? Withdrawals made before the wage earner reaches the age of fifty-nine and one-half (unless he or she becomes permanently disabled) are subject to a 10 percent tax penalty, and the amount withdrawn must be reported as income.

Senator Robert Dole of Kansas has called the IRA "the best tax break ever given the common man." The program also helps the economy by encouraging savings. Some cynics say that the IRA is necessary protection against the inevitable collapse of the Social Security system.

Inflation

is a decline in the purchasing power of money. Because of inflation, $100 hidden under a mattress at the end of 1983 bought about 4 percent less at the end of 1984.

Inflation has two causes. It can be triggered by a scarcity of essential goods—as was the case during the oil embargo of 1983–84. Businesses forced to pay more for petroleum products passed their higher costs along to the consumer.

Inflation can also be the result of the wage increases which are not accompanied by proportional gains in productivity. When this happens, labor costs per unit (of whatever a business is selling) rise. Again, businesses have no qualms about passing on increased costs in the form of higher consumer prices.

Two scales are used to measure inflation in the United

States. The Producer Price Index monitors changes in wholesale prices of food, energy products, and other commodities. The Consumer Price Index is based on retail prices and includes a broader range of items, including housing and medical care.

The "runaway" inflation, common in the late 1970s, seems to be under control in the United States: retail prices have risen at an annual rate of about 4 percent since 1983, a substantial decline from the 12 percent level of 1980. 1983 and 1984 produced the lowest back-to-back years in two decades.

Economists predict that inflation will remain in check during 1985, thanks to a strong U.S. dollar (which in turn makes foreign imports cheaper) and a world oil surplus that should keep prices of that commodity stable or even depressed.

Infrastructure

refers to the basic facilities a country needs to survive and develop—roads, schools, power plants, irrigation systems, mass communication networks, sewers, railroads, etcetera. When used in a specifically political context, infrastructure refers to the fundamental administrative apparatus which keeps it functioning.

Interferon

is a protein which prevents the spread of viral infection without disrupting normal body functions. In the bodies of humans, and most animals, an infected cell naturally produces interferon and releases it into the bloodstream.

Scientists, long aware of interferon's infection-fighting capabilities, have perfected a method for extracting the protein for use in vaccines. The process, however, is slow and costly, and thus of limited value. Recently, genetically engineered interferon has proven effective in combating a wide range of infections. The synthetic interferon is plentiful and relatively inexpensive.

In the early 1980s, interferon was thought to hold promise as a cancer treatment, but extensive testing indicated that, unfortunately, the protein has little or no effect on the growth of cancer cells.

There are several types of interferon (each kind of human cell produces its own variety) and research into its medicinal possibilities continues.

International Monetary Fund (IMF)

is a UN agency established in 1945 to promote stability in the world's currencies.

The IMF often arranges for loans to help a troubled country through financial difficulties resulting from, for example, a decline in the value of its currency and a resulting foreign debt.

Recent newsworthy IMF "rescue operations" have involved four of the world's largest debtors: Mexico, Brazil, Argentina, and Yugoslavia. In each case, the IMF persuaded foreign banks to reschedule old debts and make new loans.

IMF assistance, however, usually entails a strict austerity program on the part of the nation which has been "bailed out," and this in turn involves a lower standard of living for people, reductions in government spending and imports, and a devaluation of the nation's currency. Often there is a strong public backlash, sometimes leading to strikes, demonstrations, or riots.

In Vitro Fertilization

is a technique used to impregnate women who cannot otherwise become pregnant due to blocked or damaged fallopian
tubes or a low sperm count.

Ova are removed from the woman and fertilized with the
prospective father's sperm in a laboratory dish. The fertilized
egg is then implanted in the womb. When the procedure is
successful, the result is a "test-tube baby."

Because in vitro fertilization frequently fails, doctors routinely implant more than one embryo in the womb to improve
the chances for being impregnated. As a result, multiple births
are not uncommon in women who undergo the treatment.
Since Louise Joy Brown, the world's first test-tube baby, was
born in Oldham, England, in 1978, there have been numerous
test-tube twins, at least six sets of triplets, and one set of qua-
druplets.

By the end of 1984, almost a thousand test-tube babies
were alive and well throughout the world.

Irish Republican Army (IRA)

is an underground military organization dedicated to the unification of Ireland and Northern Ireland.

Once considered a band of noble patriots, the IRA was
formed originally by Michael Collins in 1919, as part of a movement to gain independence for Ireland. At the time, Ireland
was ruled by Great Britain. IRA guerrillas tormented British
troops (the Black and Tans) in a relentless wave of hit-and-run
ambushes and night raids. Largely because of its inability to
cope with the IRA, Great Britain eventually agreed to divide
Ireland into two separate states: the Republic of Ireland, an
independent, predominantly Catholic nation; and Northern
Ireland, comprised of six northern counties under British
(Protestant) control.

The British proposal caused a violent split in the IRA. One faction, led by Michael Collins, accepted the partitioning. Another group, called the "Irregulars," rejected the compromise, assassinated Michael Collins, and went underground. Despite being outlawed by the Irish government, the IRA continues to operate, periodically attacking British military installations in Northern Ireland.

In the late 1960s, Catholics in Northern Ireland began to protest discrimination by the Protestant majority. American journalists visiting Catholic areas in the north found living conditions comparable to the worst slums in the United States.

When Catholic protests led to bloody riots and widespread violence, British troops were sent to Northern Ireland to restore order. Fierce battles were fought between the British and IRA guerrillas for more than a decade.

Another split in the IRA occurred in 1970, and currently the organization is divided into two main factions. The "provisional" wing of the IRA is an aggressive, violent group, responsible for hundreds of bombings, assassinations, and other terrorist activities. The "official" IRA is committed to social change in the North and Ireland's unification, but rarely employs violence.

IRA provisionals rank with the world's most despised terrorists. The group has killed hundreds of civilians, including children, and, in the fall of 1984, tried to assassinate British Prime Minister Margaret Thatcher. The provisionals receive assistance from the PLO, Libya, and some Irish-Americans. Increasingly disowned by the people it claims to represent, the IRA, in the words of one editorial, has become "the darling only of the politically deranged."

Isolationism

is a foreign policy that does not favor international alliances or commitments, a philosophy whereby a nation avoids involvement beyond its borders. The term accurately describes U.S. foreign policy from 1776 until the beginning of World War I.

Today, security considerations and the growth of U.S. economic interests abroad makes isolationism impossible and undesirable. The United States needs to participate in global affairs, if only for self-protection. Still, there seems to be a growing feeling that the United States too often extends itself needlessly (sometimes dangerously). This movement toward a degree of isolationism was triggered by U.S. involvement in the Vietnam war and has reappeared in congressional disapproval of the Reagan administration's activities in Central America.

Japan, Inc.

is a term used by some American business analysts to describe Japan's strategy of close-knit national cooperation among its government, major industries, and major unions. American businessmen often see these three groups as adversaries. In Japan they are considered allies, each working for the mutual benefit of all.

Critics of the Japan, Inc. theory claim that this cooperation gives Japanese firms an unfair advantage in the international marketplace, citing the record world trade surplus that Japan has accumulated over the past decade.

Other trade experts argue that the label is no longer applicable, pointing out that while the Japanese government initially gave research and development support to selected industries, once those industries were established, government support and control ended. And government's judgment was not always infallible: it once tried to keep Honda out of the auto market and to discourage Sony from making radios.

Robert Sharp of the American Chamber of Commerce in Japan sees the whole Japan, Inc. theory as a cop out. He retorts: "Basically, we're dealing with somebody who makes a better mousetrap."

Jesse Jackson,

a Baptist minister who was once an aide to Dr. Martin Luther King, Jr., was the first black candidate for president.

Jackson said that he designed his 1984 campaign to help black Americans achieve status as an important political force and that, despite his loss, he will keep pushing for social progress.

"The movement has much to do beyond electing and being elected," Jackson said after losing the Democratic nomination. "It must expand and heal every major institution in our society."

The high point of his campaign, Jackson said in an interview, was the registration of two million voters. The low point was the total of 311 threats against Jackson's life recorded by the Secret Service.

According to a Gallup poll released in December 1984, Jackson ranks third among public figures Americans admire most, trailing only President Reagan and Pope John Paul. Jackson's supporters believe that he is a moral, religious man who is sincerely concerned about the plight of minorities and the poor. Critics see him as an opportunist who has parlayed an eloquent speaking style, and the ability to exploit a breaking news story, into national and international recognition.

In 1984, Jackson served as a diplomatic mediator, negotiating the release from Syria of Lieutenant Robert Goodman, Jr., an American airman who had been shot down over Syrian-held territory in Lebanon.

Jingoism

is a boastful, shrill superpatriotism usually accompanied by an aggressive, belligerent foreign policy. Many critics called spectator behavior at the 1984 Olympics in Los Angeles an embarrassing display of jingoism. The same charge was leveled at ABC's television coverage of the games.

Job Security,

always a concern of American workers, has recently become a higher priority than wages in many labor negotiations.

A study published early in 1985 by the Work in America Institute indicates that providing the employment security now being sought by most major unions—and extending it to all employees—may be an excellent business decision.

Higher productivity, better product quality, community approval, a more positive company image resulting in better sales, lower costs for replacing workers lost to layoffs, reduced unemployment-insurance expenses, a reduction in worker's resistance to change, and the chance to attract more able (and stable) workers are benefits accruing to firms that offer job security.

About forty U.S. companies have followed a no-layoff policy for years, including IBM, DuPont, Exxon, 3M, Motorola, Upjohn, and Control Data. The study suggests that more companies could follow this lead and use layoffs "as a last resort instead of a first choice." Even in a business decline other approaches might be tried, for example, restrictions on new hiring, early retirements, transfers, and job sharing (two employees working half-time at half-pay).

The study indicates that, even in good times, companies should use overtime, temporary employees, and subcontractors (freelancers and outside firms) to avoid overhiring, which leads to layoffs in slack periods.

Jogging Fever

is not an obsession with jogging, but an actual rise in body temperature—of about four degrees—that joggers and others who exercise strenuously experience during and after work-outs.

This "overheating" condition has been well known for some time, but two physiology researchers at the University of Michigan have now discovered that jogging fever may be beneficial. The temporary increase in body temperature (to about 102 degrees) may ward off illness in much the same way that a naturally occurring mild fever does when the body is attacked by infection.

If these findings are accurate, people who exercise regularly and experience jogging fever may become ill less often because, in effect, their exercise fever is killing budding infections in the very early stages. Researchers have already established that fever helps to fight infections by triggering certain changes in the blood that inhibit the growth of invading bacteria.

The Keck Telescope,

a gigantic "time machine" with a range powerful enough "to detect a flicker of a candle on the moon," will be built on an extinct Hawaiian volcano, officials of Caltech University announced early in 1985.

"The telescope will be able to look back in time to twelve billion years ago," said Dr. Marvin Goldberger, president of Caltech. These glimpses into long ago and far away are possible because the light emanating from distant objects left those objects billions of years ago. Astronomers will be able to see the universe in its infancy, at a time when galaxies were still forming.

The site for the Keck telescope and observatory is the 13,600-foot ridge of the Mauna Kea volcano. The location was chosen because of its dust-free atmosphere and generally cloudless skies. Construction is expected to begin in 1986. The telescope should be operational by 1992.

Caltech will spend about $85 million to build the observatory, $70 million of which will come from a grant awarded by the W. M. Keck Foundation—a charitable foundation begun in 1954 by the late oil pioneer William M. Keck, founder of Superior Oil, the world's largest independent oil and gas production company. The grant is believed to be the largest private gift ever made for scientific purposes.

KGB,

the Soviet Committee for State Security, controls the federal police and all intelligence and counterintelligence activities within the USSR. The agency's responsibilities exceed the combined functions of the U.S. CIA and FBI.

The KGB was founded in 1954 and for several years concentrated on sending political dissidents to Siberia. Recently, however, the KGB has become more concerned with intelligence gathering than systematic terrorism against Soviet citizens. (The agency still maintains an extensive network of domestic informers, however.)

According to U.S. estimates, the KGB employs 500,000 people and has an annual budget of $15 to $20 billion. Unlike the CIA, the KGB publicizes and venerates its spies, making national heroes of them. Also unlike the CIA, the KGB is firmly controlled by its government.

Kitchen Cabinet

is a term used to describe an informal group of a U.S. president's close friends and personal advisers. A kitchen cabinet can supplement or replace the formal cabinet as a president's primary source of advice on domestic and foreign policies.

The term kitchen cabinet was coined during Andrew Jackson's administration. Jackson often met with friends in the White House kitchen and often took their advice over the objections of his formal advisers.

Laser

(Light Amplification by Stimulated Emission of Radiation) is a device that converts electromagnetic energy into a highly concentrated beam of light powerful enough to burn a hole in a diamond.

Laser weapons are important components of the "Star Wars" arsenal that the Reagan administration contends is essential to the nation's defense. Many experts doubt the feasibility of laser weapons. But lasers used in U.S. Air Force tests have disabled Sidewinder missiles traveling at two thousand miles per hour.

Although these high-power lasers produce beams so potent that they can cause serious damage from a great distance, most of the lasers in use are low-power types. With reasonable precautions, they can be used safely for many purposes. Manufacturers, for instance, use lasers to cut hard materials and to weld large metal parts. In laser communications, signals are converted to pulses of laser light, allowing the clear simultaneous transmission of thousands of telephone conversations and radio/television broadcasts.

Laser surgery, an effective treatment for eye problems for almost a decade, is now being aimed at all sorts of surgical targets: lesions on the cervix and tumors on the brain, spinal cord, and bladder. Laser surgery can be done under local anesthetic, with no bleeding and no pain. Dr. Leonard Cerullo, of Northwestern University Medical School, has performed more than five hundred laser operations. "The laser is in its infancy," Cerullo said. "But in three or four years it will replace the scalpel in most delicate operations."

Latchkey Kids

are children left home alone after school while parents work. The term comes from the house or apartment keys these children sometimes wear on a chain around their necks.

U.S. Labor Department statistics indicate that in 1984 more than twenty-one million Americans with children under age eighteen are at work when their children come home from school. The estimated total represents a 15 percent increase over the previous year.

Social and family service agencies report that latchkey children, left to fend for themselves for several hours a day, have significantly higher delinquency rates than children with at least one parent at home. Latchkey kids also tend to have more problems with drugs, alcohol, and teenage pregnancy. Many don't eat or sleep properly, which affects their performance at school.

Lorraine LaSusa, the director of a phone-for-help service called Kidsline, is certain that many latchkey kids are lonely, depressed, and frightened.

"These kids are at high risk," LaSusa said, citing a 1983 case in which a ten-year-old girl, home alone, was kidnapped and murdered. "We started Kidsline soon after that killing," LaSusa said. "We regularly get calls from kids about attempted break ins. When the police check, they find that most of the calls are legitimate."

LaSusa suspects that a recent increase in the number of children reported missing in the United States has some correlation to the increase in latchkey kids across the nation. "In August 1983, there were 1.2 million missing children in the United States. At the end of 1984, that number had jumped to 1.8 million. But parents keep sticking their heads in the sand, ignoring what's happening."

After-school programs are run by several public and private agencies, but the cost, $40 to $50 per week plus transportation, is beyond the reach of many parents.

LaSusa considers that programs like her kid's help line are only "Band-aids" and believes the problems won't go away unless school districts get involved. "The situation is critical," LaSusa said. "Kids don't know how to take care of themselves, and they're being deprived of a childhood."

Leading Economic Indicators

are statistical measures of business activity that provide significant clues about future changes in the economy.

The indicators were developed just before World War II from a historical analysis of business cycles. There are thirty leading economic indicators, divided into five major groups: employment and unemployment figures; new investments; new business incorporations and business failures; stock prices; and inventory levels, spending, and prices.

Economists (and some investors) use the indicators to predict which way the economy is headed. But forecasting is not an exact science, and the indicators are subject to different interpretations.

Lebanon,

a Middle Eastern country about the size of Connecticut, lies at the eastern end of the Mediterranean Sea between Israel and Syria, a location that the U.S. and Israel consider to be vital to Mideast security.

Since Lebanon became independent in 1943, the country has relied on a delicate political balance to maintain stability. Lebanon's parliament provided proportional representation to the nation's many religious groups. Traditionally a Christian president and a Muslim prime minister worked as a team to run the government.

When civil war erupted between Christians and Muslims in 1958, the U.S. Marines were called in to restore peace, which lasted until 1969 when troops of the Palestine Liberation Organization (*see* PLO) established bases in southern Lebanon. The PLO used these bases to attack Israel. These attacks and Israel's retaliatory actions resulted in almost continuous conflict throughout the 1970s.

In 1975, a bloody civil war erupted between Christians, who opposed the presence of the PLO in Lebanon, and Muslims who supported the PLO. The fighting continued until late 1976, killing tens of thousands and ravaging the countryside. Syria, concerned about its northern borders, invaded Lebanon. Lebanon then became a fragmented nation. Syria and Druse Muslims controlled the north. The Christian government (supported by moderate Sunni Muslims) remained in power along the coast, and the south became a stronghold of Shiite Muslims and the PLO.

Tensions and conflicts between Israel and Lebanon flared again in 1981 when Israeli jets bombed Beirut in retaliation for PLO rockets fired into Israel from Lebanon.

In June 1982, Israel again invaded Lebanon, drove the PLO out of southern Lebanon and laid seige to the western section of Beirut, where remnants of the PLO army had fled. A PLO withdrawal was negotiated, and in late August, the U.S. Marines arrived to oversee the evacuation of PLO guerrillas from Beirut. The Marines withdrew on September 10th.

The PLO withdrawal did not end the violence in Lebanon, however. Christian-Muslim hostilities continued. President Bashir Gemayel was assassinated and his brother, Amin, was elected president by parliament. On September 29, the U.S. Marines landed in Beirut, joining French and Italian forces in an attempt to restore order.

Soon, Muslim terrorists began attacking the Americans. In April 1983, the U.S. Embassy in Beirut was devastated by a car bomb. Sixty-three people including seventeen Americans were killed. Six months later, a suicide truck bomb smashed through inadequate defenses and blew up Marine headquarters, killing 241 Americans and 58 French troops. In February, 1984, Druse and Shiite Muslims seized control of sections of Beirut. U.S. troops were evacuated.

During the 1984 U.S. presidential campaign, Democrats

blamed the Reagan administration for the deaths of U.S. Marines in Lebanon, and several military officials admitted that the Marines had been inadequately armed and poorly positioned.

Lebanon is a deeply troubled country, torn from within in several different directions. Its government is unstable, its economy in ruins. Foreign troops occupy much of its land. The conflicts among its religious groups are difficult for outsiders to understand, and, ostensively irreconcilable.

Most observers consider U.S. involvement in Lebanon senseless and tragic. But Israel's national wounds are much deeper. Lebanon has been called "Israel's Vietnam."

Lemon Laws

enacted in thirty-two U.S. states are basically consumer protection statutes stipulating that if a serious problem with a new car is not corrected within a specified period of time, the buyer is entitled to a full refund or another car.

Lemon laws were inspired by widespread automobile manufacturing defects which led to vigorous—sometimes violent—owner protests. A disgruntled luxury car owner, for instance, drove his defective status symbol onto the lawn of its manufacturer's headquarters and set it ablaze.

Liberation Theology

is a Catholic Social theory that has grown in response to political and economic conditions in Latin America and several other Third World countries. (See Third World) Its practice requires that the church use its influence and resources to work for a just society wherever people are oppressed. Liberation theologians are social activists, trying to create a society reflecting the dignity of the kingdom of God.

In the colonial era, Christian governments often used religion to exploit and pacify natives of Third World nations. Liberation theology, based on themes that occur often in both the Old and New Testaments, tries to correct that condition.

Pope John Paul II has frequently warned Catholic practitioners of liberation theology not to confuse liberation theology with communist propaganda. The Pope's remarks were prompted by radicals within the liberation movement who believe that violence may be moral and necessary to achieve social justice.

Libya

is located on the northeastern coast of Africa between Algeria and Egypt. Much of the country is within the Sahara Desert.

Since 1969, Libya has been ruled by Muammar el-Qaddafi (spelled Khadafy by some). Libya is rich in oil and, according to Western and Middle Eastern diplomats, Qaddafi uses the nation's wealth to subsidize terrorists throughout the world in support of a radical Marxist philosophy with which he is obsessed.

The United States closed its Libyan embassy in 1981 to protest Libya's open support of international terrorism. Later that year, U.S. jets shot down two Soviet-made Libyan fighters after the fighters attacked them in international air space. Shortly after that incident, U.S. intelligence sources charged that Qaddafi had dispatched "hit squads" to the United States to assassinate President Reagan.

In the spring of 1984, Libyan exiles demonstrating against Qaddafi outside the Libyan embassy in London were sprayed with machine gun fire from an embassy window. A British policewoman was killed and fifteen exiles wounded. The gunman returned to Libya unpunished, courtesy of "diplomatic amnesty."

Qaddafi is believed to be a madman by most of the world's civilized governments. Many suspect that Libya's president aspires to leadership of a huge African/Arab state. To substantiate their opinion, these experts point to Qaddafi's early 1985 speech during which he called upon black U.S. soldiers to desert and form their own army to overthrow the American army. He would supply the arms, Qaddafi promised. A White House spokesman called Qaddafi's statement "outrageous . . . a blatant use of racism to encourage sedition."

Line-Item Veto

is a power exercised by governors in all but a few U.S. states. The procedure allows a state's chief executive to veto sections of a bill, or individual appropriations, line by line, while signing the remainder of the bill into law. As is the case with a total veto, line-item vetoes can be overridden by the legislature.

The president of the United States doesn't have line-item veto power but some think he should, and there is a modest movement underway to propose a constitutional amendment to make it possible.

Advocates of the line-item veto believe the president should have the flexibility to approve important measures while deleting irrelevant riders, pork-barrel provisions (see Pork Barrel), and general extravagance. Opponents fear that the line-item veto would be a dangerous increase in presidential power, a procedure that would give to the executive branch legislative power which, constitutionally, belongs to the Congress.

Lithotripter

is the name of a device that pulverizes kidney stones with shock waves, and which could replace surgery for a hundred thousand patients a year.

Using shock waves similar to those generated when an aircraft breaks the sound barrier, the lithotripter reduces kidney stones to a gritty sandlike substance which can be passed almost painlessly through urination.

"What it does is an authentic medical miracle," said Margaret Heckler, Secretary of Health and Human Services, late in 1984.

The lithotripter procedure costs about $2,000 less than conventional kidney surgery (which averages $6,700 per patient). The patient is given an anesthetic, strapped into a reclining seat position, and lowered to chest level in a tub of water. X-rays are used to locate the kidney stone and focus the shock waves, which are pulsed to coordinate with the patient's heartbeat. The shock waves pass harmlessly through body tissues, but shatter the crystalline stones.

The lithotripter was invented by Dornier Systems, a West German aircraft firm. It can be used to treat 80 to 90 percent of kidney stones cases. Kidney stones afflict about one in a thousand people.

Lobbyists

are representatives of special-interest groups who attempt to influence legislation and government policy. So called because many of their contacts with lawmakers occur in the lobbies of hotels and government chambers, lobbyists testify before congressional committees and mobilize public opinion on selected issues.

Lobbying, in some form, is inevitable in a democratic society, in which conflicting views and needs compete for legislative support. The practice acquired a seedy reputation in the United States during the nineteenth century when lobbying meant buying votes with money, women, and personal favors. This reputation lingers despite strict lobbying legislation and the absence of recent scandals, but in the words of a veteran lobbyist, "Booze and broads don't work anymore and haven't for a long time."

Large special-interest groups (sometimes called pressure groups) use their memberships and resources to influence legislative opinion through information campaigns and professional presentations. The National Rifle Association (*see* National Rifle Association), the American Medical Association, the AFL-CIO, the American Farm Bureau, and hundreds of other organizations conduct extensive lobbying efforts.

Lobbyists still buttonhole legislators, in offices, hotels, bars, restaurants, and at receptions and parties. But experienced lobbyists have found that the most effective lobbying tactic is to get the folks at home involved—through letter-writing and telegram campaigns.

There are an estimated fifteen thousand professional lobbyists in Washington, D.C. Many are familiar with the inner workings of the federal apparatus. Fees for the most highly regarded lobbyists can range from $300 to $400 an hour. Often they are retained simply to keep clients advised about what's going on in the capital.

Luxury Index

is a consumer price index (*see* Consumer Price Index) for rich folks. Prepared annually by a top-of-the-line champagne distributor (with tongue firmly in cheek), the thirteen-item luxury index indicates that the cost of goods in a stylish, wealthy person's "market basket" rose 8.2 percent during 1984.

The following items contributed most heavily to the increase: the cost of a wash and cut at an exclusive New York City hair salon went up 22 percent (from $45 to $55); a mink coat selling for $11,000 at the beginning of 1984 cost $12,650 at year's end—a 15 percent increase; a pound of Teuscher Imported Chocolate Truffles, formerly available for only $22, now costs $25—up 13.6 percent; the price of a Rolex Oyster Perpetual Day-Date watch rose from $7,950 to $8,850—up 11.3 percent.

Rich-person inflation, however, is not completely out of control. The price of a Rolls Royce Corniche Convertible, Broadway theater tickets, and Hennessy X.O. Cognac all remained stable during 1984.

Magnetic Painkillers,

according to their Japanese manufacturer, relieve muscle pain. The magnets, affixed to small circular patches of adhesive material, are applied to strategic body locations and, supposedly, ease pain and stiffness by improving blood circulation.

The magnetic pain relief treatment is similar, in principle, to acupuncture and acupressure. According to Chinese medical philosophies over two thousand years old, the human body is governed by twelve energy systems, each associated with a different organ. Illness and pain, ancient Chinese theory contends, are caused by blockages in the flow of energy through these systems. Acupuncture uses needles to clear these blockages; acupressure uses massage. Likewise, the magnetic painkillers allegedly create a path for the bloodstream's energy to flow through blocked areas.

In 1984, sales of the magnetic painkillers, marketed under the label Erikiban A, reached $40.8 million. The product has been sold in Japan, and in several other Asian and European countries for several years. Early in 1985, the manufacturer of Erikiban A asked the FDA to approve sale of the painkiller in the United States.

Marian Guinn,

a thirty-seven-year-old divorced mother of four, found herself enmeshed in a modern reprise of *The Scarlet Letter*, Nathaniel Hawthorne's classic novel of puritanical persecution.

A letter read in Guinn's church denounced her for the "sin of fornication," and church elders directed the 110 members of the Collinsville, Oklahoma, congregation to have nothing to do with her.

Considerably feistier than Hawthorne's tragic heroine, Hester Prynne, Guinn refused to take the public censure lying down. She sued the church and its elders, charging invasion of privacy and "willful intention to inflict emotional distress."

In March 1984, a jury awarded Guinn $390,000 in damages. Church elders, despite being faced with the prospect of losing their church in the judgment, continued to insist that they had the "scriptural right and duty" to make Guinn's love life public.

Media Event

is a public relations device designed to attract newspaper, television, and radio exposure, and is of particular value to politicians or up-and-coming celebrities. Staged demonstrations, outrageous public statements, and bizarre stunts are all considered media events.

Medicare,

a government-backed health-care program for the elderly, was established in 1965 by the Johnson administration. The program is based on the principle that an unforeseen illness should not result in the loss of an elderly patient's life savings.

The Medicare program is considered to be in severe trouble; many experts predict it is headed for bankruptcy by 1990. The main problem is that health-care costs have skyrocketed during the past ten years and continue to rise despite the fact that inflation (see Inflation) has been brought under control.

An estimated one-quarter of all Americans have trouble paying for even routine care.

Medicare pays health-care providers (doctors and hospitals) directly, covering on the average 45 percent of an elderly patient's expenses. The program is paid for by payroll deductions and employee contributions. To make Medicare solvent, these deductions would have to be increased 40 to 50 percent.

The Reagan administration advocates cutting Medicare benefits based on the contention that the elderly have a higher after-tax income than the general population, and could afford to absorb more of their expenses than they do now. One proposal suggests that each Medicare patient should pay 10 to 15 percent of his or her income (unless the patient is below the poverty line). Supporters of this approach contend that it would make patients better "consumers" and restrict care to necessary treatment.

Other Medicare observers suggest that the health-care industry must be reined in and health-care costs brought under control. Citing surveys indicating that for every one hundred days spent in hospitals twenty are unnecessary, these Medicare reformers favor limits on the fees paid to doctors and hospitals.

Microchips

are tiny silicon wafers upon which a staggering amount of information is stored.

Collections of exquisitely miniaturized transistors can be switched on or off to transmit or block electrical current. The settings of on/off switches describes information stored on a microchip in a form a computer can "read."

The more compact the microchip circuitry, the more efficient the computer. A "bubble memory" microchip developed in 1980 is one-tenth the size of the average postage stamp and can store 8.5 million "bits" of information (eight bits are needed to store one character, whether it is a number, letter, or other typographical symbol). Smaller and smaller microchips with even greater and more efficient storage capacity are being developed.

Microsurgery

refers to a type of operation in which the surgeon views the area to be worked on through a powerful microscope. The microsurgeon uses tiny instruments similar to those employed by a jeweler in handling precious stones. Needles and probes used in microsurgery are so small they are almost invisible to the naked eye, and must be attached to long handles for the surgeon's use.

Physicians skilled in microsurgery can repair even the smallest tissues, blood vessels, and nerve fibers; they can redirect blood vessels in the brain following stroke or hemorrhage; repair damaged or clogged fallopian tubes; and revitalize paralyzed nerves. Microsurgical techniques have made it possible to reattach severed fingers, toes, or entire limbs. Shattered bones can now be mended in cases where amputation was formerly required.

Mole

is an intelligence agent (spy) who penetrates deep into an enemy nation's security or military establishment and stays undetected for years. The term originated in spy novels and was adopted for use by real intelligence operatives.

Perhaps the best-known "mole" was Kim Philby, a high ranking British intelligence officer who defected to Russia in 1963. Philby, the son of a British civil servant, attended Cambridge University and then became a war correspondent for the London *Times*.

In 1940, Philby joined the British Secret Service, eventually becoming the head of a department charged with gathering intelligence on the Russians. After his defection, Philby admitted he had been a Russian agent throughout his twenty-year career in British intelligence.

Multiple Independently-Targetable Reentry Vehicles (MIRV)

describes a ballistic missile equipped with several warheads. Each warhead (MIRV) can be aimed at up to fourteen different military targets hundreds of miles apart.

A MIRV missile need not be as accurate as a single warhead missile because it dispenses its explosives to surround the target. (See MX)

Music Videos,

filmed or videotaped performances of popular songs used as programming on cable's MTV (Music Television) and on national networks, came under attack by several groups in 1984 and 1985.

The National PTA and the National Coalition on Television Violence both complained of violence in videos, which have depicted duels, shootings, attacks on authority figures, torture chambers, bloody brawls, whippings, electrocutions, and stabbings.

The Coalition monitored three hundred hours of music videos during 1984 and found that outbursts of violence occurred, on the average, eighteen times an hour. Twenty-two percent of the videos they screened contained violence between men and women; 13 percent portrayed sadistic violence in which the attacker took pleasure. The group has called for advertising warning parents about the dangers posed by the violent video fantasies, and counter-programming of non-violent videos.

Music videos have also attracted sharp criticism from women's groups, who have noted that most of video's women are dressed in bizarre lingerie and treated as disposable sex objects.

Robert Pittman, the chief operating officer of MTV, denied that MTV is violent and dismissed the charges as being "so subjective as to be ridiculous." Pittman also rejected the notion that MTV videos are immoral or offensive.

Videos created to appeal to an older, more conservative audience are gaining broader distribution through an increasing number of outlets. Soft rock, mild rhythm and blues, and pop-country presentations are being offered to adults who are uncomfortable with the style and substance of MTV fare.

MX (Missile Experimental)

is an ICBM missile weighing 190,000 pounds. It carries ten high-yield (extremely destructive), high-accuracy atomic warheads and has a range of six thousand miles.

The MX has a long, controversial history. It was originally conceived in the 1960s as a MIRV missile with sufficient mobility to render it invulnerable to Soviet attack. The MX languished in the drawing-board stage, remaining a gleam in the defense industry's eye, until 1979, when the Carter administration approved its full-scale development.

The controversy surrounding the MX focuses on two issues: its cost (over $200 million per missile) and method of deployment. Carter's deployment plan involved placing two hundred MX missiles on underground shuttles that would keep them in constant motion through a network of 4,600 shelters. The plan was discarded due to high cost and opposition from the western states where the shelters would have been located.

President Reagan favors the MX and has offered several suggestions for its deployment: in "dense packs" (clusters of MXs in fortified silos); "deep basing" (in silos so deep they are invulnerable); and in ABM (Anti-Ballistic Missile) defended silos.

MX supporters claim that the missile is needed to reduce Soviet ICBM superiority, and as a bargaining tool in arms control talks. Some MX critics favor hundreds of smaller, single-warhead ICBMs, moved frequently to confuse Soviet intelligence.

In March, 1985, President Reagan urged Congress to move ahead with the MX missile, arguing that the MX (which Reagan has nicknamed "Peacekeeper") is vital to U.S. security and the success of arms control negotiations.

National Organization for Women (NOW)

was founded in 1966 to achieve "full equality for women in truly equal partnership with men." Feminist author and activist Betty Friedan was NOW's first president. Headquartered in Washington, D.C., NOW has eight hundred local groups and about 130,000 members, making it the largest civil rights organization in the world.

NOW's major campaigns have been directed toward eliminating prejudice and discrimination against women. It uses the courts, lobbying, boycotts, and demonstrations to achieve its goals, strongly supporting, for example, The Equal Rights Amendment (which failed to gain ratification).

NOW endorsed Walter Mondale in the 1984 presidential election, charging that President Reagan's lack of commitment to Affirmative Action and women's rights issues made him an unacceptable chief executive.

National Rifle Association (NRA)

was established in 1871 for people interested in the sport of shooting. The NRA has over 1.8 million members including hunters, gunsmiths, gun collectors, police personnel, and target shooters.

An exceptionally vocal lobby (*see* Lobbyist), the NRA wages a relentless and effective campaign against gun-control legislation from its headquarters in Washington, D.C. Since 1968, the NRA has persuaded Congress to reject major gun-control bills fourteen times, despite opinion polls indicating that a majority of the American public favors such legislation.

National Sales Tax

is a proposed federal tax on consumer purchases added on to the sales tax now in effect in most states.

Proponents of a national sales tax believe it would raise federal revenues to levels at which income taxes could be greatly reduced or, perhaps, eliminated completely. Advocates claim that a national sales tax is preferred over income taxes by a two to one margin, and would raise $25 billion for each percentage point of tax.

Most national sales-tax plans envision a procedure in which the tax would be collected at the retail level as some state and local sales taxes are now. The national sales tax would "piggyback" other sales taxes and be passed along to the federal government by the states (which would keep a piece of the action for their trouble). There would be no exemptions for necessities such as food and medicine.

Critics of a national sales tax say that such a tax would place an unfair burden on the poor, who spend a higher percentage of their income on necessities.

National sales tax proponents believe that the tax would

be easy to collect, would encourage savings and investments, and discourage reckless spending.

Near-Death Experience

is a term used to characterize the reports of thousands of people who either came very close to death or actually were, for a time, clinically dead.

Scientists have found a common pattern in people's recollections of the near-death experience. a sense of extreme peace and well-being, a feeling of separation from the body, the ability to "gaze down" at the body from some higher vantage point, and movement through a dark space (much like a tunnel) to encounter a warm brilliant light. In a number of cases, people reported seeing deceased relatives or friends, and sometimes a religious figure.

According to researchers, about one-third of adults who come close to death report the near-death experience. The experience does not seem to be limited to any particular type of person. Age, sex, physical condition, or religious orientation seem to have no bearing. (An atheist is just as likely to report the experience as a deeply religious person.)

People who report the near-death experience usually change their lifestyles afterward. Many claim that they are more relaxed, enjoy life to a fuller extent, and have blossomed spiritually.

Scientists have not concluded that the near-death experience proves the existence of an afterlife. It does seem to suggest that the moment of death is not to be feared.

Neutron Bomb,

a relatively small atomic weapon, has been considered for use in battlefield (tactical) situations.

A hydrogen bomb releases its destructive energy through radiation, intense heat, and a powerful blast. The neutron bomb, however, produces less heat and blast but emits considerably more radiation—in the form of neutrons.

Neutrons, because of their composition, travel great distances and pass through most matter. The human body, mostly water, is highly susceptible to neutron radiation—which is deadly.

The neutron bomb was designed primarily for use by NATO forces in the defense of Western Europe. It can be launched with the short-range Lance missile, or as an artillery shell.

Critics of the neutron bomb say it makes atomic war too feasible. Some call it the ultimate weapon of a capitalist society: it kills people but leaves property intact.

Proponents of the neutron bomb, including former President Jimmy Carter, argue that more people would die in a full-scale nuclear war than in defensive battles in which the neutron bomb was used to repel invaders.

Nicaragua,

originally a Spanish colony, is the largest and least populous of the Central American nations. Nicaragua gained its independence in 1838 and first attracted serious United States attention in 1903, when Marines were dispatched there to secure territory for a potential canal between the Atlantic and the Pacific.

When two U.S. citizens were assassinated in Nicaragua in 1909, U.S. policymakers switched their preferred canal site to Panama, where a canal was completed in 1914. U.S. Marines continued to occupy Nicaragua, however—first to prevent foreign companies from establishing a competing canal, and later to conduct surveys for a potential second canal.

The lingering presence of the Marines provoked the rise of a nationalist movement led by a guerrilla (see Guerrilla) leader, César Augusto Sandino. Despite continued efforts to stifle his revolutionary movement, Sandino swore he would continue his fight, and not emerge from his mountain hiding place until the Marines left.

The Marines did leave in 1933. Before doing so, however, they armed and trained a Nicaraguan national guard and appointed as its leader Anastasio Somoza García.

Sandino, true to his word, emerged from hiding. He and his brothers were immediately murdered on orders from Somoza, who then established a dictatorship continued by his heirs for the next forty-two years.

Nicaragua reemerged in the news in 1979 when a popular revolutionary movement led by the "Sandinistas" (see Sandinistas) deposed Anastasio Somoza Debayle, Somoza Garcia's son.

By 1981, tension between the United States and the Sandinist government had become critical. The Reagan administration cut off aid to Nicaragua on grounds that the Sandinistas were "exporting revolution" in partnership with the Soviet Union and Cuba.

In addition to withdrawing aid, the Reagan administration took several active measures aimed at weakening and eventually ousting the Sandinist government. Counterrevolutionary guerrillas called contras (see Contras) received millions of dollars in covert assistance from the Central Intelligence Agency (see CIA). In early 1984, Congress ordered a halt to such aid after learning that the contras had mined Nicaraguan harbors damaging several foreign ships, including a Soviet freighter.

Throughout the controversy, the Sandinistas have denied that they are exporting revolution. In early 1985, however, they admitted receiving substantial amounts of Soviet-built weapons, tanks, aircraft, and assorted military equipment for "defensive purposes."

Norplant

is a five-year contraceptive injected underneath the skin of a woman's upper arm. In 1985, the U.N. World Health Organization (*see* World Health Organization) found the contraceptive to be safe and effective, opening the way for its worldwide use. The U.N. agency believes the contraceptive may be essential for population control efforts underway in dozens of developing countries.

The implant, manufactured by a Finnish pharmaceutical firm, was tested on fourteen thousand women, including eight hundred residents. Already in use in Sweden and Finland, the contraceptive costs $30–$60. Norplant is as effective as sterilization but its effects are immediately reversed when the implant is removed.

The FDA (*see* FDA) has begun its own Norplant testing and is expected to approve the contraceptive for sale in the United States by 1987.

North American Air Defense Command (NORAD)

consists of tracking stations around the world linked electronically to about ninety huge computers deep inside Cheyenne Mountain in Colorado. The purpose of the system is to warn the U.S. military in the event of an attack.

About twenty years ago, NORAD built tracking stations in strategic locations all around the globe. Each tracking station has a powerful telescope focused on a specific section of the sky. Mechanisms inside NORAD telescopes change light and shadow to electronic signals which can be analyzed by computers at the tracking station. This analysis can identify an object the size of a basketball from 20,000 miles away.

Information gathered by NORAD tracking stations is transmitted to Cheyenne Mountain headquarters, where it is projected on huge screens. NORAD experts immediately decide if an object detected by one of the tracking stations is a danger to the United States.

NORAD headquarters are located fourteen hundred feet

underground behind doors of steel and concrete weighing twenty-five tons. There are fifteen office buildings inside Cheyenne Mountain, where about seventeen hundred people work in NORAD's underground city.

North Atlantic Treaty Organization (NATO)

consisting of Belgium, Canada, Denmark, France, West Germany, Greece, Italy, Luxembourg, the Netherlands, Norway, Portugal, Spain, Turkey, the United Kingdom, and the United States, is a mutual defense pact established in 1949 primarily to deter potential Soviet aggression in Europe. A key provision of the agreement which created NATO is that an armed attack against any NATO member is to be treated as an attack against all.

NATO's main concern is maintaining a military balance with its Soviet-controlled counterpart, the Warsaw Pact (see Warsaw Pact) nations. From its headquarters in Brussels, Belgium, NATO also handles questions of strategic polling (the credibility of nuclear deterrence, for example), works for standardization of weapons and equipment among its members, and tries to resolve political disputes between NATO allies (conflicts in recent years, for example, between Greece and Turkey).

Nuclear Regulatory Commission (NRC)

is a federal agency established in 1975 to assure that civilian uses of nuclear materials and facilities are consistent with public health and safety standards.

During 1984, the NRC was frequently charged with violating the regulations it was created to enforce. Most members of the commission, said James Asselstine (himself an NRC member), "tend to view their job as protecting the industry rather than the public."

During 1984, several controversies arose involving the NRC, most notably the Diablo Canyon case (see Diablo Canyon). Here, the NRC ignored the possibility that the plant's location near an earthquake fault might complicate emergency planning. Another case involved the Grand Gulf nuclear plant in Mississippi. After its operating license was issued, hundreds of errors were discovered in the data used to make the licensing decision—yet the NRC allowed the plant to continue operating.

Nuclear Winter

is a term used by many scientists to describe the horrible climatic effects of atomic war.

Although Richard Turco, a California researcher, coined the phrase (in 1983), West German atmospheric chemist Paul Crutzen was the first to visualize and validate the nuclear winter scenario.

Using a computer to simulate a war involving about half of the world's nuclear arsenal, Crutzen found that fires ignited by atomic warheads would burn for several weeks, releasing about 400 million tons of soot into the atmosphere. The smoke from thousands of fires would merge into a thick dark cloud cover spanning most of the northern hemisphere and blocking out as much as 99 percent of the sun's light. Temperatures would plummet sixty degrees or more for several months. Plants, animals, and even plankton would die. Any rain would be harshly acidic. When the soot settled, it would drop to earth, and with it, tons of radioactive particles.

Crutzen's insight inspired extensive research throughout the scientific community, and the news about nuclear winter has gotten worse. Stanford biologist Paul Ehrlich predicted that vicious storms, spawned by extreme temperature differences between land and sea, would ravage coastal waters, making fishing impossible. Other scientists discovered the "quick freeze," a deep sudden chill which would occur within two days of even a small nuclear explosion. University of Colorado researcher John Birks reported that toxic substances (including PCBs and dioxins) released into the air as cities burned, could be even more deadly than nuclear winter's severe cold.

Nuclear winter specialists hope that their discoveries will put an end to the threat of nuclear war. These scientists believe that they have proven that a nation launching a major nuclear attack would be destroying itself—and most of the world—even if not a single missile is ever fired in retaliation.

But there are skeptics, among them Edward Teller, developer of the hydrogen bomb. Teller contends that the effects of nuclear winter could be managed if nuclear war occurred in real winter, and if only military targets were hit, with relatively small warheads. Others doubt the premise upon which nuclear winter is based, or dispute the accuracy of environmental models used in the computer calculations which verified the concept.

While only nuclear war can completely validate the nuclear winter theory, its proponents stand by their calculations. A 1950 forest fire in western Canada, they note, produced smoke visible in Europe, and for two days absorbed half of Washington, D.C.'s sunlight.

"Interest in nuclear winter is low, even among anti-nuke groups," Paul Crutzen admitted late in 1984. "It sounds so strange, I don't blame them. I think the timescale for public awareness of nuclear winter is very long—several years."

Even if the military superpowers accept the inevitability of nuclear winter, scientists worry that a shift to space weapons or neutron bombs (see Neutron Bomb), which produce less fire and more radiation, may be the only result.

Occupational Safety and Health Administration (OSHA)

is a regulatory agency within the Department of Labor. Created under a 1970 law that requires employers to furnish their employees a workplace free from hazards to life or health, OSHA enforces comprehensive industrial safety regulations which must be adhered to by all employers.

Organization of American States (OAS)

is a regional political body whose membership includes the United States, Mexico, and most of the countries of Central and South America. Its concerns are the maintenance of peace in the Western Hemisphere and the settlement of disputes within an inter-American arbitration system. Since the 1960s, economic cooperation has risen to become a top OAS priority.

The OAS is composed of a General Assembly (which meets once a year) and several councils. The organization has been involved, to some extent, in all major political problems of its region.

The OAS reluctantly approved U.S. intervention in the Dominican Republic (1965), expelled Cuba (1962), and condemned the invasion of Grenada by the United States and other OAS members (1983).

In general, the OAS opposes U.S. domination of Latin American affairs, but is not militantly anti-American.

Office of Management and Budget (OMB)

is an agency within the executive branch of government. Each year, the OMB reviews spending proposals of all federal agencies, determines whether or not funding requests are compatible with presidential programs, and drafts a budget which the president then sends to Congress.

The OMB was formerly the Bureau of the Budget, which was established in the Treasury Department in 1921 and moved to the president's office in 1939. The agency prides itself on its "neutral competence," or efficient performance regardless of which party is in power.

In addition to budgetary functions, the OMB is responsible for the administration, organization, and coordination of the day-to-day operations of the executive branch of government. It participates in most major presidential decisions and serves as an information body overseeing the work of most, if not all, principal federal agencies. It tends to attract the best civil servants, who generally stay with the agency for many years.

Organization of Petroleum Exporting Countries (OPEC)

was founded in 1960 in Baghdad, Iraq. It is a cartel, an organization of nominally independent commercial enterprises designed to control oil prices and thus to limit competition.

For a seven-year period, starting with the oil embargo of 1973–74, OPEC maintained steady, annual increases in the price of crude oil. In the early 1980s, reduced demand for oil and increased production by non-OPEC members, coupled with political unrest among several of the OPEC nations, slowed and finally reversed the oil price spiral.

As a result, oil prices fell about $2 a barrel in 1984 and are expected to fall another $2 to $4 by the end of 1985. This should return oil to its 1979 price of $25 per barrel.

Additionally, OPEC's "poorer" members (Algeria, Ecuador, Gabon, Indonesia, Iran, Iraq, Nigeria, and Venezuela) have depleted the funds they accumulated during the boom period; their combined indebtedness now totals $76 billion. More important, they need whatever oil revenues they can get and so are reluctant to take part in the production cuts and price wars that richer nations (Kuwait, Libya, Qatar, Saudi Arabia, and the United Arab Emirates) often initiate.

Economic experts note that OPEC's inability to stem declining oil prices improves the United States' economic outlook, keeps the inflation (*see* Inflation) rate low, reduces interest rates, and triggers economic growth.

"The weak links in the chain are close to breaking," reported a 1985 study commissioned by Wall Street financial analysts. "There will be a decline in oil prices as the financial pressures of the weaker members intensify."

Paleolithic Diet

Two Atlanta researchers conducted exhaustive anthropological studies of prehistoric man's eating habits and concluded that the key to health in the 1980s may be the menus of 40,000 B.C.

In a 1985 article published in the *New England Journal of Medicine*, the researchers theorized that many modern diseases, including stroke, heart failure, and some forms of cancer have spread because man is eating food incompatible with his caveman genes.

According to the article, a diet of high-protein, low-fat meat would keep modern man as lean and mean as his prehistoric ancestors.

Although the authors of the article meant for their findings to be taken seriously, medical and media reaction suggested that the premise of the Paleolithic Diet was a little goofy. Cavemen stayed thin, it has been suggested, because they spent more of their lives chasing animals than eating them.

Palestinians

The establishment of Israel, shortly after World War II, divided what had been the Arab-Jewish nation of Palestine into a Jewish state (Israel) and an Arab state (now Jordan). The partitioning of Palestine, and the Arab-Israeli war which broke out immediately after, dislodged a large number of Palestinian Arabs. A small number of these Palestinians were absorbed by neighboring Arab nations. The overwhelming majority, however, ended up in refugee camps in Jordan, Israel, and Egypt. These Palestinians and their descendants created what one historian has called "the festering sore of the Middle East."

The plight of Palestinian refugees over the last several decades has become the focus of several Arab-Israeli conflicts. Since 1948, Palestinians have been demanding the return of their homeland and creation of a Palestinian nation.

In the early 1960s, several guerrilla groups seeking to liberate Palestinian areas from Israeli control formed the Palestine Liberation Organization (PLO). In 1964, leaders of Arab nations in the Middle East declared that the PLO was the official political representative of all Palestinians in the region.

Al Fatah, the largest guerrilla group within the PLO, gained control of the organization in 1969. Al Fatah's leader, Yasir Arafat, became the PLO's president and chief spokesman.

Initially, the PLO was based in Jordan. But by 1970, the organization had become too powerful there ("a state within a state," one Jordanian official complained). War broke out between the PLO and Jordan. Despite the support of Syria, PLO bases were destroyed and the guerrilla group was driven out.

The PLO reemerged in Lebanon, a troubled nation lacking the unity to prevent PLO domination of selected areas in its southern regions (bordering Israel). Beginning about 1970, the PLO launched a campaign of international terrorism culminating in the murder of Israeli athletes at the 1972 Olympic Games. World reaction to the incident caused the PLO to denounce all terrorism outside Israel.

In 1973, a major split in the PLO occurred. So-called moderates, led by Arafat, stated that they would accept a Palestinian homeland limited to an area west of the Jordan River. Radicals remained firm in their belief that Israel must be eliminated and replaced by a nonsectarian Palestine where Muslims, Jews, and Christians would share in the government.

Over the past six to seven years, the PLO has fallen into disarray. Israelis routed PLO forces in Lebanon in 1978 and again in 1982. The organization is now split into a half-dozen factions which, though they agree that a Palestinian state must be established, differ dramatically in how to achieve that goal. (*See* Lebanon)

Papua, New Guinea,

a nation of 3.4 million people in the eastern half of the island of New Guinea, is considered to be one of the most primitive societies on earth. It is largely populated by aborigines still living in a Stone Age culture.

Yet Papua has made steady progress since gaining its independence from Australia in 1975. The new nation is coping well with modernization despite widespread poverty, migration to urban areas, and massive culture shock.

An encouraging report is provided by Australian teachers who report that Papua youngsters are quick to learn and grasp sophisticated ideas and technological skills. They comment that some of the children "are going to make the leap from the Stone Age to the Nuclear Age in a single generation."

Participative Management,

a relatively new management style used by hundreds of U.S. businesses, involves employees in their company's decision-making process.

Participative management is an attempt to meet employees' needs, partly from a commitment to human development and partly from a desire to increase workers' productivity. The concept originated in part from a 1969 study at the University of Michigan, which showed that most of the 1,533 workers interviewed ranked interesting work and personal authority ahead of either good pay or job security.

Advocates of participative management point out that it improves the quality of many business decisions, leads to greater acceptance of company goals and policies, and creates a level of teamwork found only in Japanese industry (*see* Japan, Inc.).

Critics of participative management point out that there often isn't enough time to get everyone involved in hundreds of decisions, and that the process can lead to antagonism and conflict between workers and management.

In practice, participative management seems to work best in small to medium-sized companies in which most employees are skilled professionals or technicians.

Party Animals—

the Democratic donkey and the Republican elephant—became party "mascots" through the political cartoons of Thomas Nast.

During Andrew Jackson's presidential campaign, his opponents frequently referred to him as "a jackass." Nast, followed quickly by other political cartoonists, began using the donkey kicking the stuffing out of various opponents as a party symbol.

Nast was also responsible for the Republican elephant. In 1874 Nast drew an elephant charging toward victory and trampling Democratic opponents along the way. The symbol stuck and, like the Democratic donkey, remains a party symbol to this day.

PCP,

an animal tranquilizer also known as "angel dust," is, tragically, the drug of choice for thousands of American teenagers.

PCP is inhaled, injected, swallowed, but more often smoked (often mixed with marijuana) by young people who are attracted by the vivid hallucinations and the sense of weightlessness they experience during the average six-hour PCP "trip." Aftereffects include panic, extreme paranoia, and a sense of despair. These side effects render the drug quite dangerous. Murders and freak accidents, such as teenagers leaping from buildings in the belief that they could fly, have been attributed to the drug.

Perks,

short for perquisites, are fringe benefits of a job—everything from paid insurance and stock options to a company car and tropical junkets.

Privileges and "fringes" are important elements in the compensation packages U.S. corporations offer to attract top executives. For many companies, the total cost of these perks may be equal to one-third of all payroll expenses. For the executive receiving them, the real value of perks is that most are tax free.

The perkiest jobs in the country may be those held by members of Congress. Among the freebies federal legislators enjoy (in addition to their annual salaries of $72,200) are generous staff allowances (up to $1.5 million per year), free furnished offices in Washington and back home, unaudited expense accounts ($200,000 annually, on the average), subsidized travel (including free hospitality at U.S. embassies), unlimited free phone calls, sizeable pensions after five years of service (with automatic cost-of-living adjustments), free health club facilities, cut-rate barber and beauty treatments, subsidized private dining rooms, free legal counsel, postage, calendars, photography services, maps, pamphlets, potted plants, and steep discounts at special stores.

This mountain range of goodies is, of course, not free; U.S. taxpayers pick up the tab. Congressional mail privileges alone add up to $100 million a year.

Persian Gulf,

an extension of the Arabian Sea, lends its name to the oil-rich region along its shores. The Persian Gulf nations include Iran, Iraq, Kuwait, Bahrain, Saudi Arabia, Oman, and the United Arab Emirates.

Since war broke out between Iran and Iraq in 1980, the Persian Gulf region has become a world trouble spot. The security of the region is of vital interest to the United States and the Western world. About 7.5 million barrels of the world's highest-quality oil is shipped through the Persian Gulf daily. There is considerable concern that the Iran-Iraq conflict will disrupt that flow of the industrial world's most essential commodity.

The prime concern of Persian Gulf leaders is that Iran will defeat Iraq and "destabilize" its neighbors. "If the Iraqis crumble, the whole area will crumble," a United Arab Emirates official predicted. Gulf states fear that Iran will "export revolution," and support terrorism throughout the region.

Confidence in the United States as a source of protection has dwindled recently because of the Marines' withdrawal from Lebanon (see Lebanon), the White House's failure to bring about peace in the Mideast, and the feeling that the Reagan administration too heavily favors Israel. Further evidence that the United States is "unpredictable" came in 1984 when American missile sales to Jordan and Saudi Arabia were canceled.

The United States maintains a strong naval presence in and near the Persian Gulf and President Reagan has warned that there is "no way" that the United States will allow oil traffic to be disrupted.

The Peter Principle,

coined by author Laurence Peter in his 1969 bestseller of the same name, states that ". . . in a hierarchy, every employee tends to rise to his level of incompetence." Since Peter published his findings, media writers, business people, and ordinary workers have discovered thousands of new examples and illustrations to support Peter's hypothesis.

Philippines,

formerly a U.S. territory, spans seven thousand islands scattered over five hundred miles off the southeastern coast of Asia. Only about fifty of these islands are bigger than one square mile and only about 4,800 of them have names.

Since 1965, Ferdinand Marcos has been president of the Philippines. His reelection in 1969 came after a campaign marked by violence and fifty-nine deaths. Widespread protest against Marcos's repressive government led to more unrest in 1971 when armed conflicts resulted in about five hundred deaths. Marcos declared martial law in 1972, and ruled the Philippines as a military dictator for the next eight years. In 1977, the U.S. State Department issued a protest strongly critical of human-rights violations committed by the Marcos regime.

Marcos ended martial law in 1980 and was reelected president. Most opposition parties boycotted the election. Later, opposition leader Benigno Aquino (a former legislator) was shot to death in Manila as he returned from exile. Within large segments of the Philippines population there was considerable suspicion that the Marcos government was involved in the murder. The Aquino assassination sparked huge anti-Marcos rallies and hundreds of violent clashes between demonstrators and police.

For several years, armed opposition to the Marcos regime

has been led by the New People's Army (NPA), a Communist guerrilla force of about ten thousand, which controls 20 percent of the Philippines. The NPA cultivates a Robin Hood image, claiming it is fighting oppressive landowners and resisting injustice. The NPA's biggest ally in its fight for control of the Philippines is, ironically, the Marcos regime itself, which fuels the growing unrest by its brutal treatment of dissidents and insensitivity to pleas for democratic reform.

The situation in the Philippines is being watched closely by U.S. officials. In 1985, the Pentagon asked Congress to double military aid to the "deteriorating" nation. Asking for a $100 million appropriation, Secretary of Defense Casper Weinberger said, "We are deeply concerned. The rapidly growing Communist insurgency presents a serious problem." According to the Defense Department, the Philippine army is badly neglected, and some units have to forage for food and use palm oil to lubricate their weapons. Patrols keep in contact with each other through runners because they have no radios. The Pentagon believes that the disarray in the Philippines poses a direct threat to U.S. security, because there are no real alternative locations for the American military bases which have been established there. About fifteen thousand troops are stationed in the Philippines.

Strategic needs aside, the excesses of the allegedly democratic government of Marcos are embarrassing to the United States, which has repeatedly requested that the Philippines open its political process. Minimal progress has occurred.

In the election of 1984, Marcos supporters retained control of the National Assembly, but opponents—a group of small parties united only in their hatred of Marcos—realized signifi cant gains.

Piggies

are annual "awards" given to the nation's most sexist advertisers by the feminist (see Feminism) Women Against Pornography (WAP) group. In 1984, Piggy winners included:

- Calvin Klein—for an underwear ad showing a woman with her back arched and her T-shirt rolled up to expose her breast, in a pose the group declared "straight out of *Penthouse.*"

- Huggies Diapers—for an ad presenting little girls "in cheesecake poses" which ignores the prevalence and seriousness of child molestation.

- HippOppoTamus—for a boot advertisement that "glamorizes macho aggressive behavior."

Pioneer 10,

a spacecraft launched in March 1972, is now more than 4 billion miles into the Milky Way.

Called by many the space program's most successful launch, Pioneer 10 is the only object ever to leave our solar system. It weighs 565 pounds and travels at 30,500 miles per hour.

The craft is expected to roam the universe for 100 billion years. Pioneer 10 is, in a sense, an ambassador from earth to the rest of the universe. Attached to its hull is a gold "greetings" plaque engraved with the likeness of a man and a woman, as well as a space map showing the way to earth.

Plastic Sea Litter,

primarily from broken or discarded fishing nets, is choking the world's oceans, which are already polluted with oil spills, toxic chemicals, and radioactive wastes.

According to marine scientists, plastic is killing millions of birds, fish, whales, sea turtles, and seals. Some die after becoming entangled in pieces of plastic nets; others after eating small pieces of indigestible plastic. The problem is serious and, in 1985, more than 150 wildlife researchers met in Honolulu for an international conference to study solutions.

The National Academy of Science estimated that each year commercial fishing fleets dump more than 52 million pounds of plastic packaging into the sea, and lose 298 million pounds of plastic fishing gear. The Entanglement Network (fourteen conservation groups) presented evidence that 1 to 2 million sea birds, and more than 100,000 sea mammals (including whales, dolphins, and seals) die yearly because of plastic litter.

Plastic fishing nets (most made in Japan) are cheaper to produce, but unlike twine or other net material, plastic is not biodegradable. Environmental groups are pushing for international legislation to restrict or outlaw plastic debris in the world's oceans.

Pocket Veto

The president is allowed to consider a bill passed by Congress for ten days before he must sign it into law or exercise his powers of veto. If Congress adjourns before the ten days allowed for the president's decision has expired, the president can, in effect, veto the bill by doing nothing ("putting the bill in his pocket").

The president need not cite any reason for his pocket veto, and the veto cannot be overriden by Congress.

Because the pocket veto gives the president complete control over all bills passed within ten days of adjournment, Congress makes every effort to pass important bills early in the session.

Political Action Committee (PAC)

is an organization through which special-interest groups contribute campaign funds to candidates who support their positions.

More than 3,100 PACs were in operation in 1984. They contributed more than $100 million to candidates for congressional seats. PACs can represent a fairly wide range of interests (a labor PAC) or have a single-issue orientation (a pro-Israel PAC).

PAC opponents are convinced that special-interest groups use their campaign contributions to buy—or at least rent—members of Congress. Groups such as Common Cause have attempted to demonstrate a correlation between the PAC contributions legislators receive and the votes they cast. While it has been difficult to establish any direct evidence of PAC influence on lawmakers, the appearance of impropriety is common.

Supporters of the PAC concept claim that the committees allow individuals to pool their resources and thus have a greater impact on a candidate's positions. They also point out that the proliferation of PACs, promoting a wide diversity of opinion, tends to minimize the influence of any single PAC. Finally, PAC proponents note, legislators' votes are ultimately determined by factors far more powerful than PAC influence, namely, party affiliation, ideology, and constituent opinions.

Political Spectrum (Left, Moderate, Right)

In the French General Assembly, during the eighteenth century, the monarchists and conservative noblemen sat to the presiding officer's right. Radical populists sat to the presiding officer's left. Separating the two factions (who tended to attack each other physically, given the opportunity) was a group of moderates, seated in the chamber's center, directly in front of the presiding officer.

Today, the terms right, left, and moderate (or middle of the road) are used to categorize political philosophies and styles of government, and are loosely based on those two-hundred-year-old seating arrangements.

Polychlorinated Biphenyls (PCBs)

are a chemical waste produced in numerous plastics manufacturing procedures. Although illegal since 1978, thousands of tons of PCBs are produced annually, and released into the world's atmosphere and water supply.

The toxic waste kills or contaminates birds, fish, and other wildlife, can cause a human ailment called Yusho disease which affects the skin, eyes, and internal organs, and which can cause bone deformities. Laboratory tests have linked high PCB levels to birth defects and cancer. PCB contamination has rendered the Hudson River in New York and other waterways useless for fishing. Environmentalists are not sure PCBs can ever be removed from riverbeds or lake bottoms. Many experts believe that PCBs have become the most widespread chemical pollutant.

Late in 1984, waste disposal researchers suggested that specially selected bacteria might be the cheapest way to control PCB pollution. A pilot program at the University of Wisconsin used strains of bacteria to break down PCBs into harmless carbon dioxide and water. The method, which reduced PCB contamination by 60 percent, would cost only one-fifth as much as incineration—the only currently approved PCB disposal technique.

In 1985, the Environmental Protection Agency levied a $6.8 million penalty—the largest toxic waste penalty in history—against Chemical Waste Management, Inc., of Oak Brook, Illinois, alleging that the toxic waste disposal company illegally discharged high levels of PCBs into waste lagoons to dilute them and thus avoid federal regulations requiring burning of the wastes. After dilution, the EPA complaint charged, more than six million gallons of the contaminated liquid were sold as reclaimed oil.

Populism

is a political movement dedicated to fulfilling the needs of the "common people." Deeply ingrained in U.S. tradition, populism is considered democratic radicalism or liberalism of the masses. In the 1890s, a formal Populist party existed nationally (a coalition of farmers and labor unions).

In recent times, the populist label has been used by politicians believing themselves to be champions of the "little guy." Governor George Wallace of Alabama claimed to be a populist.

In tax reform debates, attempts to simplify the tax code and redistribute the tax burden more fairly are often referred to as populist proposals.

Pork Barrel Legislation

provides federal funds for local projects (often of dubious value) designed to keep senators and congressmen in the good graces of their constituents.

The pork barrel is, metaphorically, the federal treasury. Legislators of both houses—and both parties—dip into it to finance fish hatcheries, to secure bailouts for cotton farmers, to widen highways, to build military bases, etcetera. Pork barrel projects range from extravagant water diversion networks to senseless defense contracts—all justified on the grounds that they provide employment "back home."

A 1984 White House survey on cost control indicates that pork barrel legislation adds billions of dollars annually to the federal budget. For example, Senator James McClure (R-Idaho) sponsored a $9.3 million program to subsidize the education of mining engineers at a time when there was no demand for them.

Other heavy-duty pork purveyors identified in the White House survey were Senator Robert Byrd (D-West Virginia), Representative Tip O'Neill (D-Massachusetts), Senator Ted Stevens (R-Alaska), Senator Dennis DeConcini (D-Arizona), and Representative Silvio Conte (R-Massachusetts).

Precinct

is the basic political unit in the U.S. electoral process. All American cities and counties are divided into precinct polling districts, each containing two hundred to one thousand voters. The structures of both major political parties is built along precinct lines. Each party appoints or elects a precinct captain who functions as the party's leader in dealing with voters within that precinct. The precinct captain is expected to work year round getting voters registered, doing political favors, doling out jobs, and carrying on routine party business. Precinct captains go to a lot of wakes, attend school and church functions, sponsor picnics—whatever it takes to stay close to the precinct's voters.

Above all else, the precinct captain is responsible for getting his party's voters to the polls on election day. Organization at the precinct level is vital to a political party's success, especially in cities where large numbers of voters are often concentrated within a few blocks.

Prime Rate

is the interest rate that banks charge their best corporate clients. Rates available to other businesses are usually quoted in relation to this rate ("two points over prime," for example).

Analysts of the economy often use the prime rate as a

gauge to determine if business activity is likely to expand or slow down. A relatively low prime rate usually means that businesses can get all the money they need to grow. A high prime rate means that money is tight, which usually makes expansion too costly.

Prisons for Profit

More and more private businesses are winning government contracts to operate penitentiaries and jails. The trend toward prisons for profit is growing because, for most states, counties, and municipalities, the concept is economically attractive.

For years, penal authorities have paid private organizations to operate halfway houses where prisoners near the end of their sentences were fed, housed, and prepared for reentry into the community. In 1982, the state of Florida turned over the operation of a state prison for four hundred juveniles to a private company. Soon after, authorities in Tennessee and Texas contracted with private firms to run prisons in those states.

Prison entrepreneurs can run penal institutions more efficiently than government agencies because they are more flexible in hiring and firing, procuring supplies, and general administration. The private companies seem to be more adept at operating job-training programs in prisons, and several have arranged jobs for convict labor forces (an approach which earns money for the inmates and for the prison entrepreneurs).

Three out of four corrections officials oppose the prisons-for-profit concept. They doubt that required services can be delivered at the prices quoted by prison entrepreneurs, and fear the liability the state would incur if private guards mistreat inmates. Prison workers' unions also oppose the idea, contending that private firms will hire less qualified workers at lower rates of pay.

Probable Cause,

a legal requirement for a valid arrest or lawful search and seizure, is the existence of substantive evidence that a crime has been committed.

Whether or not law enforcement officers have probable cause to search or arrest a suspect is always decided by a judge. Probable cause can be established in several ways: by relying on the cumulative knowledge of police officers, physical evidence, the testimony of witnesses, or a tip from an informant. The fact that a suspect has been involved in similar crimes in the past is of little value in trying to establish probable cause.

Pro-Choice

is the label given to those who support the right of women to decide for or against abortion. The pro-choice position holds that a woman's decision is private, beyond the control of law or government.

Unlike right-to-life (see Right-to-Life) advocates, pro-choice supporters accept a Supreme Court decision which, in effect, has decreed that a fetus does not become human until the seventh month of development. Right-to-life advocates believe that the fetus becomes human at the moment of conception.

Pro-choice groups resent what they call the "emotionalization" of the abortion issue and the heavy-handed "scare tactics" employed by some right-to-life supporters, claiming that an already traumatic choice for most women is being made more difficult. Citing the tragic consequences that unwanted pregnancies often bring to women, children, and society, the pro-choice movement demands that women who choose to consider abortion be left alone.

Most pro-choice advocates condemn "abortions of convenience," in which abortion is used as a birth control tech-

154

nique. Supporters of the pro-choice position typically propose education and freer access to contraception information and materials to reduce the number of unwanted pregnancies, especially in the young and the poor.

Protectionism

is a national foreign trade policy to restrict imports, or tax them to increase their price. Supporters of the policy say that it is necessary to protect American business and the jobs of U.S. workers from foreign competition. Opponents claim that protectionism inspires retaliation against U.S. exports by foreign governments.

Quasars

located at the center of every galaxy, are the most luminous objects in the universe, burning with the brightness of a *trillion stars.* The energy required to produce the light emanating from quasars has caused a scientist to call them "the ultimate celestial powerhouse." To date, the origin of quasars is unknown, as is the source of their astounding energy.

Racewalking,

a new form of rapid walking somewhere between walking and running, gained popularity in the mid-1980s. According to an increasing number of exercise experts, racewalking has all the benefits of running with none of the risks.

Its advantages include a low incidence of injury (the hip

action keeps the torso moving forward at one level with no bouncing up and down), ease of performance, efficient weight control, and long-range cardiovascular benefits. It can be pursued throughout one's life; champion racewalker Edward Weston walked from San Francisco to New York in seventy-seven days at age seventy-one.

The fastest racewalkers can cover a mile in six minutes and sustain a pace under eight minutes a mile almost indefinitely. Racewalking is catching on; racewalking clubs are now forming all over the United States and many former runners are among their numbers.

Radial Keratotomy (RK),

is a new and controversial surgical procedure designed to correct myopia (near-sightedness). In a RK operation, which costs about $1,500 and takes only minutes to complete, the surgeon cuts into the surface of the eye, making seven tiny incisions in the cornea (which looks like a spoked wheel when the procedure is finished). When successful, the surgery allows the patient to see things they were unable to see before without glasses.

More than sixty thousand RK operations have been performed in the United States, but the rave reviews of patients have not convinced all eye surgeons that the operation is safe or necessary.

The RK operation was developed in 1975 by Dr. S. N. Fyodorov, a Soviet ophthalmologist. A Detroit eye specialist learned the procedure from Fyodorov and performed the first radial keratotomy in the United States in 1978.

The National Eye Institute views RK surgery suspiciously, implying that doctors who use it are "fast buck" artists, or misguided scientists utilizing human eyes as research tools.

The demand for RK surgery far exceeds the supply. The number of eye surgeons who perform the surgery is limited and they choose their patients carefully. RK is an extremely delicate procedure. The surgeon must cut as deeply as possible into the cornea without cutting all the way through. Helpful in reducing the danger of the surgery are the ultrasonic pachymeter, which measures the thickness of the cornea accurately, and the diamond blade scalpel, which can be set to lengths measured in fractions of a millimeter. Even so, the cornea is only about one-half millimeter thick and a certain amount of courage is needed to request the operation.

Complications occur in one out of a thousand operations. Many eye doctors feel that even this low risk rate is unacceptable when operating on essentially healthy eyes. RK is cosmetic surgery, these doctors contend.

Recession

is a period of economic hard times less severe than a full-fledged depression. During recessionary periods, major industries stop expanding and may even decline. The GNP (see GNP) declines and there are fewer jobs and lower wages. Spending drops sharply also, and inventory does not move, either at wholesale or retail levels.

Author and social historian Ben Wattenberg insists that recessions are "as American as apple pie" because they occur with regularity. His study of U.S. economic history in the post-Civil War period shows that recessions occur periodically, as pauses in long-term economic growth. According to Wattenberg, such fluctuations seem to be departures from a constantly ascending line of growth: down two steps and up five; down five steps and up seven. From 1970 to 1983, per capita income rose 28 percent. The poverty rate was 22 percent in 1960; by 1983 it had dropped to 8 percent.

Since the end of World War II, the average recession in the U.S. economy has lasted about eleven months; the average decline in industrial production has been about 10 percent. Recessions have been as mild as the one in 1960, and as severe as the one of 1981–1982, which lasted longer and was more serious than any other economic setback since the Great Depression of the 1930s.

Redlining

is the illegal practice of denying mortgages or building improvement loans because of the location of the dwelling. Charges of redlining are often leveled against lending institutions that have a record of refusing funds to purchasers of homes in urban ghettos and other low-income areas. In effect, redlining acts to deny loans to racial and ethnic minorities.

Congress has tried to discourage redlining by requiring lenders to publicize where their funds are distributed and by adopting a series of anti-redlining regulations. Opponents of redlining claim it is the major cause of urban decay, because without the backing of banks and other lending institutions, efforts to rebuild crumbling city neighborhoods are doomed to failure.

Lenders deny that their loan procedures are discriminatory, contending that they shouldn't be forced to make loans to irresponsible applicants, or for buildings in areas where it is impossible to obtain fire or hazard insurance.

Regressive Tax

is any tax in which the burden of payment falls too heavily on low-income taxpayers. A regressive tax is the opposite of a progressive tax (such as the U.S. income tax) in which the tax rate rises as income increases.

Most sales taxes are considered to be regressive because they take a higher percentage from the total income of the poor than the middle income or the rich. Sales taxes on food, medicine, and other necessities of life are probably the most regressive of taxes; a major portion of the money earned by low-income families must be spent on these kinds of goods. (*See* National Sales Tax)

Referendum

is the referring of legislation to voters for final approval or rejection. The process limits legislative power by reserving the final say on certain laws for the electorate.

Most states use the referendum process; the federal government does not. The kinds of laws which cannot be passed without a referendum are generally listed in a state's constitution. Usually, these include amendments to the state constitution, the imposition of certain kinds of taxes, and local governments borrowing (through bond issues) for services such as schools, libraries, and roads.

Revenue Sharing

is the return of federal tax revenues to state and local governments. These revenues are not subject to the controls and supervision associated with other federal grants. The idea of revenue sharing was proposed by the Kennedy administration, but not implemented until 1972 by President Nixon.

Distribution of revenue-sharing funds is based on a congressionally calculated formula that considers each state's population, tax structure, and relative per capita income. State and local governments determine how and when funds will be spent. Since its inception, critics have charged that the revenue-sharing program frequently allocates funds inequitably.

The Reagan administration's 1985 budget proposals would sharply cut revenue-sharing funds.

Reye's Syndrome

is a rare, usually serious, and often deadly disease contracted by children. During the early 1980s, six hundred to twelve hundred cases per year were reported in the United States. In 1984, 190 cases were reported.

Typically, Reye's Syndrome occurs as the child is recovering from the chicken pox or the flu. The disease strikes suddenly with high fever, severe headaches, vomiting, and central nervous system disorders. The usual symptoms are sometimes followed by convulsions and coma.

Research at the Atlanta Center for Disease Control has established a possible link between Reye's Syndrome and aspirin. In response to government urging, most major United States aspirin distributors, early in 1985, voluntarily agreed to label their products with a warning publicizing the suspected danger.

Reye's Syndrome has a 25 percent mortality rate and has resulted in several cases of severe brain damage. The disease is named for R.D. Reye, the Australian pathologist who first identified the disease in 1963.

Sandinista

is the popular name for the ruling political party in Nicaragua. The party, formerly a guerrilla force, is named for César Augusto Sandino, a popular anti-American revolutionary and guerrilla leader of a nationalist movement begun in 1927.

Sandino's goal was to drive U.S. Marines from Nicaraguan territory. In 1933, he and his followers succeeded. Their victory was short-lived. In 1934, troops trained by U.S. personnel and led by General Anastasio (Tacho) Somoza Garcia assassinated Sandino and overthrew the Liberal government that Sandino had been instrumental in forming. A military dictatorship was installed by Somoza and passed along to his heirs.

In 1979, leftist guerrillas launched a civil war to over-throw the government of Anastasio Somoza Debayle, Somoza Garcia's son. The guerrillas called themselves Sandinistas. (*See* Nicaragua)

Right to Die

is a national movement dedicated to upholding a terminally ill patient's right to voluntarily discontinue the use of artificial life-support systems.

A patient's right to "self-determination," right-to-die advocates insist, is constitutionally guaranteed. Early in 1985, a California appeals court affirmed that position.

William Bartling, a seventy-year-old Californian suffering from five diseases, all considered fatal, tried unsuccessfully to be disconnected from a respirator at the Glendale Adventist Medical Center. Bartling sued to be allowed to die naturally but lost.

Six months later, the appeals court overruled that decision, stating that "the right of a competent adult to refuse medical treatment is a constitutionally guaranteed right which must not be abridged."

Courts in New Jersey, Florida, Delaware, New York, Washington, and Massachusetts had previously decided that terminally ill patients should be allowed to decide if they wanted their lives sustained artificially, and "living will" laws have now been passed in twenty states.

Ironically, Bartling died the day before his case reached the appeals court, making that court's ruling an empty victory.

"They just prolonged his dying," Bartling's wife Ruth said. "I wasn't going to win and my husband wasn't going to win because he was always going to die. At least there will be guidelines for other people in the future."

A Glendale Adventist hospital spokesperson said the hospital was seriously considering an appeal to the California supreme court. "We are concerned that the decision accords no rights to the physician and hospital in this kind of confrontation," said the spokesperson. Hospital attorneys had argued that removing Bartling from life-support systems amounted to aiding a suicide.

Right to Life (or pro-life)

is a label applied to the hundreds of anti-abortion groups active in the United States and around the world. Right-to-life advocates believe that abortion and infanticide are morally identical. "Absolutists" within the movement oppose abortion under any circumstance; moderates would allow the procedure if the fetus were seriously deformed, if the mother's life were in danger, or if the pregnancy was the result of rape or incest.

Abortion was legalized January 22, 1973 when the Supreme Court overturned a Texas law prohibiting the procedure. During the first six months of pregnancy, an abortion can be performed for any reason. The procedure is illegal in the final three months (the third trimester) of pregnancy, except when necessary to save the mother's life, because it has been determined that the fetus is "viable" (able to live outside the womb) at this stage of development. In the United States, 93 percent of the 1.5 million abortions performed annually occur during the first three months of pregnancy; less than 2 percent in the final trimester.

Right-to-life advocates believe that a fetus becomes a human being at the moment of conception, which, in their eyes, makes abortion murder. Groups within the right-to-life movement use emotional appeals to state their case, distributing literature depicting aborted fetuses piled in garbage cans and characterizing abortionists as "head crushers" and "baby killers." During the year ending January 1985, two dozen abortion clinics were bombed.

More than seventy thousand members and supporters of the right-to-life movement marched to Washington, D.C., on January 22, 1985, protesting the anniversary of abortion's legalization. Pro-life obstetrician, Dr. Bernard Nathansan, presented to government officials a videotape of an abortion called *The Silent Scream.* The tape shows an abortion procedure during which a twelve-week-old fetus was supposedly struggling and grimacing, its mouth open in a "silent scream."

Critics of the videotape claim that a twelve-week-old fetus lacks the nervous system development required to feel pain and call the tape an exercise in "crude emotionalism." Similar charges have often been leveled against the right-to-life movement, even by those who support the movement's basic position on abortion.

President Reagan openly supports most right-to-life objectives, but seasoned political analysts suspect that Reagan's support is mostly symbolic, noting that Reagan has done little to bring about a constitutional amendment (called the Paramount Human Life amendment) to outlaw abortion.

Abortion is a visceral issue with deep moral and religious undertones. Compromise seems impossible. As President Reagan has observed, "Abortion is either the taking of a life or it's not. If it is—as medical technology increasingly seems to indicate—it must be stopped."

Pro-lifers, to date unsuccessful in launching a constitutional amendment prohibiting abortion, note that five Supreme Court justices are in their seventies, presumably nearing retirement. If two of these justices step down, as the right-to-life movement hopes, replacements appointed by President Reagan could change the court's position on abortion.

Robotics

In science fiction, robots are metal humanoids—usually stumpy and clumsy—who talk in beeps and whirs and run into walls. In real life, the robotics industry has built hundreds of cleverly engineered machines designed for a number of specialized industrial functions.

Most robotic devices are self-propelled, self-steering, and

equipped with a limited memory system for storing instructions and making simple (yes-no) decisions. Many robots have hand-arm attachments with which they can determine the hardness, size, temperature, distance, and positions of the objects they handle.

The thousands of industrial robots in use today (about half of them in Japan) load machine tools, spray paint cars, do spot welding, and perform foundry and assembly-line functions.

Salad-Bar Sulfites,

food preservatives often sprayed, tossed, or sprinkled on salad-bar foods to keep vegetables looking fresh, may be harmful to asthmatics and others, health officials reported in 1985.

An allergic reaction to salad-bar sulfites has been linked to four deaths, and the Food and Drug Administration (*see* FDA) is investigating over fifty reports of adverse reactions which include diarrhea, itching, nausea, swelling of glands, hives, unconsciousness, and shock. Asthma sufferers seem to be the most severely stricken.

The FDA has requested that warning signs be posted in restaurants which use sulfites to preserve food. Physicians suggest that anyone who thinks he or she is allergic to sulfites should ask the restaurant manager if the preservative is being used.

Sanctuary Movement,

a loosely knit organization involving an estimated 170 U.S. churches and synagogues, is dedicated to helping Central American refugees escape the oppression and violence of their native lands.

The sanctuary movement made news early in 1985 when the U.S. government indicted sixteen sanctuary movement members—including two Roman Catholic priests, three nuns, and a Protestant minister—charging the group with violating several immigration laws. If convicted, each faces a $10,000 fine and prison sentence of up to five years.

U.S. government officials and critics of the sanctuary movement maintain that the clergy and laity involved in this movement are naive; that they are simply helping illegal aliens to greater economic opportunity, counter to restrictions imposed by the Immigration and Naturalization Service.

Sandwich Generation

describes an increasing number of Americans "caught in the middle"—raising their children while simultaneously trying to care for elderly parents.

According to Purdue University Professor Marsella Smith, "More and more of us are going to find ourselves in this caretaker situation because people are living longer. Researchers are telling us now that by the year 2020, people over the age of sixty-five will outnumber teenagers by two to one."

Smith observes that few people realize the community resources available to the elderly. "So the adult child tries to do it all himself and winds up feeling overburdened, frustrated, resentful, and guilty."

The chief concern of the "sandwich generation," Smith believes, is coping with elderly relatives moving in. The key to establishing the best relationship possible in this situation is to make the older person feel useful.

"We love them, want to make life easy for them, and we end up making them more dependent," Smith notes. "Then it gets to where we ourselves can't cope and we holler for help."

Help is available in most communities, and through other family members, Smith advises. "We're seeing many more day-care centers for the elderly."

Saturn

will be the first new General Motors car line since the Pontiac in 1926. GM will establish an entirely new company—Saturn Corporation—to produce the compact cars.

Early in 1985, GM chairman of the board Roger Smith called Saturn "the key to long term competitiveness, survival, and success." The goal of Saturn is to make cars comparable to Japanese autos in both quality and cost.

Saturn cars, GM estimates, could be in showrooms by 1988 or 1989. GM plans to build a huge factory (four-million square feet) to produce Saturn cars, and create twenty to forty thousand new jobs in the process. The half-million Saturns to be built each year will come in two models—a four-door sedan and a two-door coupe. The cars will be priced at around $8,000.

Except for an ignition lock that is built into the floor-mounted gearshift instead of the steering column (making the car tougher to steal), not much about the Saturn is unusual. The real innovation is in the way the care will be produced. GM, borrowing techniques from Toyota, will use robots and computers on the assembly line. Computer controlled assembly will reduce manufacturing mistakes and significantly cut down production time.

The competition for Saturn assembly plants is intense, involving almost every state in the union. GM has been besieged with offers of tax breaks, government-backed loans, and other incentives. Because of the jobs it will create—including those in spin-off parts industries—a Saturn plant is viewed, in the words of one state official, as "the biggest industrial prize of the generation."

School Prayer

In 1984, a moment of silence "for meditation or voluntary prayer" allowed in public schools in twenty-three states was declared unconstitutional by a federal court. John Baker, attorney for the state of Alabama, disagreed with the decision and promised to appeal to the Supreme Court. Baker called the moment of silence a "common sense accommodation to the religious diversity of our people," and said it was not unconstitutional because no religion was endorsed.

Agnostics who had sued to stop the moment of silence contended that when public school teachers (state employees) say that prayer is permissible, the state is promoting religion.

In dispute is the constitutional requirement for strict separation of church and state. Although clear to constitutional scholars, the separation doctrine has sometimes caused controversy when it is upheld.

Seabed Mining

In the 1870s, scientists discovered that wide areas of the ocean floor were teeming with valuable minerals. Yet one hundred years passed before major efforts to extract seabed minerals were launched.

For the past several years, scores of international miners and petroleum exploration experts have cooperated in deep-sea mining ventures. It is a costly enterprise and the technology is uncertain. Even so, explorers believe that the world's seabeds are rich in industrial treasures. International laws allowing for the filing and exploitation of seabed "claims" are expected to be worked out by 1986.

Search Warrant

is an order issued by a judge authorizing law enforcement officers to conduct a search of specific premises for things or persons specified in the order.

A search without a warrant is illegal unless it occurs during an arrest, in a "hot pursuit" situation, or with consent.

A judge will not issue a search warrant unless the police establish probable cause. If issued, the warrant will describe exactly which areas police are permitted to search, and what they may seize.

Sexual Child Abuse

Reports of sexual child abuse in the United States increased sharply in 1984, more than doubling in many states. According to a survey released by the National Committee for Prevention of Child Abuse, 123,000 new complaints were recorded during the year ending in December 1984.

Experts believe that, despite the increase in reports and a rising public awareness of the problem, the bulk of sexual child abuse remains undetected. Several studies of adults suggest that almost half of females questioned and a third of males were sexually abused while growing up.

Several major prevention programs were launched recently, including a special Spider Man comic strip in which Spidey discloses that he was abused as a child and urges children similarly violated to report abuses.

Most sexual child abuse involves relatives, family friends, or other adults the victim trusts. More often than not, sexually abused children are afraid or ashamed to report the abuse, and many convince themselves they are somehow at fault.

Sidewinder,

an air-to-air missile, is used extensively by the United States, all NATO countries, and several other American allies. The Sidewinder comes in several versions; all have heat-seeking or radar-directed homing devices. The missile, about nine feet long and five inches in diameter, is used in air combat. (See Star Wars)

Recently, a prototype laser weapon (see laser) shot down a Sidewinder missile in mid-air—the first evidence that so-called Star Wars weapons may have practical potential.

Siege Mentality

is a phrase used to describe a pervasive fear of crime, which has led thousands of Americans to arm themselves or otherwise alter the way they live.

According to a report issued by the Eisenhower Foundation in 1985, violent crime in the United States has increased dramatically over the past fifteen years—to levels which are "astronomical" compared with crime rates in other industrial nations. One of every three American households is touched by a major crime in an average year.

Researchers have found that 40 percent of U.S. citizens are so fearful of attack that their lives are being affected even if they have never been victimized. Women routinely carry guns, icepicks, and tear gas in their purses. Self-defense classes are flourishing in many communities.

Law-enforcement officials, in some cases, are becoming concerned that there are too many guns in the hands of people who will be unable to use them. Criminologists doubt that most middle-class Americans could shoot an attacker without hesitation, or live with themselves afterward if they did.

Siege mentality is making fortresses of U.S. homes and creating a current of paranoid tension that is straining the social fabric and ruining lives, psychologists say.

Positive suggestions for reducing crime and alleviating the atmosphere of terror it creates include building stronger family neighborhood ties and working to increase cooperation with police. Neighborhood-watch programs, in which residents of the community become the eyes and ears of the police force, have been cited as examples of crime-prevention techniques that work without resorting to vigilantism.

Sikhs

India's 14 million Sikhs are a religious minority whose beliefs and customs are a synthesis of Islam and Hinduism. Over the past few years, the sect has become militant, demanding autonomy for Punjab, the Indian province that the Sikhs dominate.

The Sikh religion was founded by Guru Nānak in India in the sixteenth century as a way of making peace between warring Hindus and Muslims. Sikhs are monotheistic, focusing their faith on a series of gurus whose instructions and philosophies are set down in the Sikh's holy book, the *Granth Sahib*. Sikhs, whose religion decrees the wearing of swords, consider themselves "holy warriors."

In a day-long battle on June 6, 1984, the Indian army attacked hundreds of Sikh militants in the Golden Temple of Amritsar, the holiest of Sikh shrines. Supported by mortars, antitank rockets, and heavy machine-gun fire, army regulars killed almost 1000 Sikhs, among them charismatic leader Jarnail Singh Bhindranwale. The attack on the Sikh shrine was ordered by India's Prime Minister Indira Gandhi.

The Sikhs retaliated on October 31, 1984, when two of Gandhi's Sikh bodyguards assassinated her as she walked from her residence to a nearby garden where she was to have been interviewed. Anti-Sikh rioting spread through all of India after Gandhi's assassination. More than twenty-seven hundred people were killed, most of them Sikhs.

Anger at the Sikhs still exists in India, despite the efforts of Prime Minister Rajiv Gandhi (Indira Gandhi's son) to defuse tensions.

Sikhs have thrived in India as professionals, businessmen, merchants, and property owners. As a group, Sikhs are among the most prosperous Indians.

Slush Fund

describes money (usually unreported) collected by politicians for personal use. Although federal and state laws require that all campaign funds be accounted for, slush-fund money seldom finds its way into the accounting process.

One of the most peculiar slush funds ever uncovered belonged to former Illinois Secretary of State Paul Powell. After Powell's death, shoeboxes containing almost $2 million were found in his hotel room.

Small Business Administration (SBA)

is a government agency that makes direct loans to small businesses and guarantees loans made by private lenders. The SBA also offers small business an extensive array of management-training programs.

In 1985, the Reagan administration advocated what amounts to the virtual dismantling of the SBA. Administrative budget proposals would effectively abolish the SBA's loan and guarantee powers and almost all of the agency's management-training programs.

The SBA does not seem to be doing much good, the administration contends, noting that about eleven thousand small businesses fail each year, a mortality rate eight times higher than that of large firms (over $1 million in annual revenue).

According to business experts, under-capitalization and inefficient management are the primary causes of small business failure. Many contend that if the SBA—a major source of funds and training—is abolished, thousands more small firms will disappear, taking the jobs and competition they now provide with them.

Space Mausoleums

A consortium of U.S. undertakers and space engineers has announced plans to begin rocketing the remains of thousands of people into orbit. For $3,900, the Celestis Group will place a dearly departed's ashes in space to rest in cosmic peace for infinity.

According to surveys commissioned by the space burial firm, interest in the concept is more than sufficient to make the business profitable. Space Services of Houston, Texas—a firm headed by former astronaut Donald Slayton—will supply the rockets, which will carry six to thirteen thousand burial capsules per launch.

Each burial capsule will be two inches long and about a half inch in diameter. If requested, a cross, a Star of David, or other religious symbol would be added to the name and social security number to be placed in each capsule. The surface of the capsules will be highly reflective, so that loved ones with high-powered telescopes can watch the deceased pass overhead on clear nights.

The burial capsules will be placed nineteen hundred miles above the earth, out of the way of other spacecraft and thus not considered "space clutter."

The Department of Transportation gave its approval to the space mausoleum proposal in early 1985. The Celestis Group has begun taking "flight reservations."

Standard of Living

is the level of life's necessities and comforts to which a person, social class, or citizens of a nation are accustomed.

Like the gross national product (GNP), a nation's standard of living is an indicator of economic health. National standards of living are usually compared through their per capita incomes, a nation's income divided by its population. Switzerland's per capita income in 1980 was $16,440; Ethiopia's was $140.

Star Wars

is the media label for the Strategic Defense Initiative (SDI), a system of space-based defensive weapons still in the early development stages.

President Reagan supports the SDI concept enthusiastically but dislikes the "Star Wars" connotation. "I wish whoever coined that expression would take it back because it gives a false impression of what we're talking about," he has said.

What we *are* talking about, according to scientists, is a system which might include speed-of-light lasers, particle-beam weapons, and high-velocity railguns that will fire lethal projectiles at incoming missiles.

Proponents say that the SDI system may one day make nuclear arsenals obsolete. Critics of the proposed system say it is too expensive ($26 billion in research costs, to start), not scientifically feasible, and likely to lead to the militarization of space. Critics also claim that SDI violates the 1972 SALT agreement.

State Department

(also the United States Department of State) is the cabinet-level organization charged with the conduct of U.S. foreign affairs. The department is headed by the secretary of state, usually the president's principal adviser in foreign policy.

The exact role of the secretary of state depends on the personality and philosophy of the president. Some presidents (Franklin Delano Roosevelt, for example) are, in effect, their own secretary of state.

Normally, the secretary of state assists the president during international crises and in diplomatic affairs by presenting all elements of an issue, optional causes of action, a broad survey of world opinion, and his own views and recommendations.

The State Department negotiates treaties, represents the United States in foreign countries, recommends and implements foreign policy, and attempts to promote understanding and acceptance of U.S. policies throughout the world.

The State Department includes a Policy Planning Council to analyze and propose the future course of American diplomacy. Under State Department jurisdiction is a network of about three hundred embassies, legations, consular posts, and special missions. Specialized regional bureaus, each headed by an assistant secretary of state, conduct the department's day-to-day work. There are five regional bureaus: European Affairs (which includes Russia and Canada); Inter-American Affairs; African Affairs; Near Eastern and South Asian Affairs; East Asian and Pacific Affairs. A separate bureau guides the U.S. participation in the United Nations and other international organizations.

The State Department's Agency for International Development is responsible for administering nonmilitary aid to foreign countries. This includes funding for loans, grants, education, research, and development. The State Department's headquarters, nicknamed "Foggy Bottom," are in what was once a swamp near the Potomac River, an area frequently beset by fog.

Sterile America

According to government figures, more than half the married couples in the United States are unable to have children. A study released early in 1985 by the National Center for Health Statistics reported that the sterility rate for couples had reached 52 percent, more than double the 1965 level. Surgical sterilization for purposes of birth control was cited as the cause of the dramatic increase.

Edging past birth control pills, elective surgical sterilization has apparently become the most popular method of contraception for U.S. couples. Two procedures are most common: men are sterilized by vasectomy, a simple operation which can be done in a doctor's office. Women desiring sterilization must go though a more complicated procedure—a tubal ligation.

SALT (Strategic Arms Limitation Talks)

There were two SALT agreements in which the United States and the Soviet Union agreed to place limits on certain nuclear weapons.

SALT I was signed in Moscow in 1972 after three years of negotiations. Its two major provisions included a five-year agreement to limit offensive strategic (ICBM) weapons and the number of launchers for nuclear missiles; and a treaty of indefinite duration limiting defensive antiballistic missiles (ABM) to one hundred per side.

SALT II, signed in Vienna in 1979 but never ratified by the United States Congress (because of the Soviet invasion of Afghanistan), limits each side to 2,250 ICBMs. Despite the failure to ratify, both the United States and the Soviet Union agreed to abide by the provisions of SALT II. There is evidence, however, that neither side did so. SALT II expires in 1985.

Strategic Arms Reduction Talks (START)

were an extension of the SALT (see Strategic Arms Limitation Talks) treaties negotiated by the United States and the Soviet Union from 1972 to 1979.

The arms reduction talks began in 1982 in Geneva, Switzerland. The United States proposed that each side reduce nuclear warheads by one third. The Soviets said they might consider this if the United States would forgo deployment of new medium-range missiles in Europe and restrict cruise missile development and deployment.

As negotiations unfolded, some observers claimed that the USSR's main goal was to limit U.S. cruise missiles while continuing to develop their own. (The Soviets were thought to be five to ten years behind the United States in cruise-missile technology.)

START discussions abruptly ended when, after the United States began deploying intermediate-range Pershing II missiles in Western Europe, the Soviet negotiators left in protest.

Street People

are the nation's homeless—three million men and women living in doorways, subway tunnels, abandoned cars, and garbage dumps.

The homeless population, already at its highest level since the Depression, is increasing as low-income housing continues to vanish and mental institutions accelerate the mainstreaming of patients unable to fend for themselves.

Federal funds for the homeless are presently limited to $60 million ($20 per street person), and organizations such as the Salvation Army find themselves overwhelmed with two to three times the people their facilities were built to accommodate. Cities and charitable organizations are joining forces to build shelters, but are meeting resistance from citizens' groups who fear that some of the homeless may be violent, posing a threat to children.

According to some estimates, the ranks of the street people will continue to swell—at a shocking rate of 10 percent a year.

Student Loans,

guaranteed by the U.S. government and offered at interest rates below market levels, came under close scrutiny as 1985 budget-cut proposals began to take shape.

The student-loan program has several features which increase its cost. The government must pay banks the difference between the student loan's bargain interest rate (5 to 8 percent) and market rates (12 to 14 percent), and until the student graduates, the government pays *all* interest on the loan. Adding to the program's cost is a high rate of delinquency. Defaults have doubled over the past four years. Graduates who go on to lucrative careers in law, medicine, or business are stiffing the government for about $2 billion a year, which rankles the program's opponents almost as much as it infuriates taxpayers.

"I know of no program which so clearly and on so large a scale imposes costs on low-income people to provide subsidies to high-income people," said economist Milton Friedman.

Proposals to restructure the student loan program include lowering maximum family income level at which loans will be made available, and ending the hefty interest rate discounts. According to Reagan administration officials, the changes will make it clear that while the government will help needy students get an education, the student will share the cost more equitably.

Opponents of the proposed cuts say the decrease in student loan availability will hurt students and colleges, place a heavy burden on middle income families, and make it increasingly difficult for lower income families to meet escalating college costs.

Subway Vigilante

is the label assigned Bernhard Goetz, an electronics engineer, who, on December 22, 1984, shot four black youths on a New York subway after they allegedly tried to rob him.

Although no one was killed in the incident, one of the youths Goetz shot was paralyzed and rendered comatose. Goetz was arrested for attempted murder, but after substantial public support for his actions became obvious, was indicted only on a weapons charge by the grand jury (see Indictment) assigned to the case.

In the view of many observers the massive outpouring of public support Goetz received demonstrated increasing grassroots sympathy for crime victims and provided dramatic evidence of the public's toughening attitute toward crime and criminals. (All the youths involved in the incident were awaiting trial on criminal charges.)

While some officials called reaction to the Goetz case "a referendum on the breakdown of the criminal justice system," others in the law-enforcement community worried that the subway vigilante's actions would encourage a "Dodge City mentality"—thousands of citizens packing guns on the streets of U.S. cities. "Some people are going to try to read into what happened here as a kind of license to shoot anybody who looks mean," New York Governor Mario Cuomo said.

As anyone who has seen a couple of westerns knows, vigilantes assume law enforcement powers whenever they see the need to do so, often going beyond the boundaries of self-defense to mete out swift (but not always just) punishment. President Reagan hoped that the Goetz incident would not lead to a rash of vigilantism. "I can understand the frustration of people who are constantly threatened by crime . . . but I realize there is a breakdown if people start taking the law into their own hands."

In February 1985, C. Vernon Mason, representing the youth paralyzed in the Goetz incident, filed a $50 million civil suit against the subway vigilante. Mason charged that Goetz, driven by racial hatred, "went out looking for a black kid to shoot . . . armed to the teeth—at Christmastime—with 'dum-dum' bullets." Mason claimed that Goetz had continued firing as the youths attempted to run away, and that, after the shooting, Goetz was overheard uttering racial slurs and expressing a desire to gouge the youths' eyes out. Mason, in press conferences, called Goetz a bigot, and described the massive public support the subway vigilante received as violent racism.

Several black leaders disagreed with Mason's charges, saying that Goetz's actions were understandable, and that blacks, more susceptible to street crime than whites, were fed up with being victims and generally supported Goetz. Dr. Willard Gaylin, an urban psychologist, also rejected the racism charge saying that the public's reaction to the shooting indicated community anger and fear, not racial hatred.

Four days after the grand jury refused to indict Goetz for attempted murder, a black Chicago plumber shot and killed a knife-wielding black teenager who tried to rob the plumber in the street. Chicago police declined to bring charges.

On March 27, 1985, Goetz was indicted by a New York City grand jury on charges which included attempted murder, assault, and reckless endangerment. The Manhattan grand jury refused to make public the "new evidence" which resulted in the indictment, but newspapers published portions of Goetz's original statement to police which seemed to weaken his self-defense claim.

According to these accounts, Goetz told police he "checked" the bodies of the four wounded youths, and seeing no blood on one of them, said, "You don't look so bad; here's another," as he fired his gun into the youth's ribs.

Sudan

In northeast Africa, the largest country on the continent (population 20.6 million) is considered to be critical to the U.S. defense efforts in the nearby Middle East because of its proximity to Egypt. With the possible exception of the Philippines, no U.S. ally is suffering from deeper political and economic difficulty.

Since 1969, Gaafar Nimeiri (sometimes spelled Nimeiry) has been president of Sudan's military republic. In 1972, Nimeiri had succeeded in uniting the Arab Moslems of North Sudan with the black Christians of the south. For reasons no informed observer could understand, Nimeiri reversed himself in 1983. First he divided the south into three separate provinces (apparently to play southern leaders off against each other). Soon after, he declared a form of Islamic law for all of Sudan, including the Christian south. Finally, Nimeiri denied the south's request for its own oil refinery.

Nimeiri's actions sparked a vicious civil war. Southern rebels, calling themselves the Sudan People's Liberation Army, have created havoc in Sudan. In some areas, support for Nimeiri has eroded to the extent that entire units of the Sudanese army are defecting.

In July 1984, Nimeiri charged that neighboring Ethiopia and Libya—with the assistance of the Soviet Union—were waging a secret war in Sudan, encouraging dissent and unrest and supplying rebel troops. In February 1985, U.S. Vice-President George Bush went to Sudan to try to convince Nimeiri to put his nation back together again or risk the loss of $250 million annually in U.S. economic and military aid.

On April 6, 1985, Nimeiri was overthrown in a bloodless coup led by his defense minister, General Abdel Rahman Siwar el-Dahab. The coup followed more than a week of mass protests and general strikes sparked by actions Nimeiri had taken which resulted in high food prices.

The new government assured the United States, Egypt, and Saudi Arabia that Sudan would remain a committed ally.

Sunbelt

is the popular name for the band of southern states extending from Virginia to Florida and west to California. This U-shaped configuration of states is characterized by mild climate, favorable tax structures, and labor laws generally attractive to industry. As a result, it is the section of the country experiencing the most dramatic growth today.

Since 1980, over 90 percent of U.S. population increases

have been concentrated in sunbelt states. A major trend has been the relocation of manufacturers from northern and midwestern industrial states (dubbed by some as "the rust belt") to sunbelt states. Ironically, the mass migration of industrial workers who followed in industry's wake created major unemployment problems in such suddenly overpopulated states as Texas: industrial facilities are not built overnight, and jobs didn't materialize fast enough to take care of the streams of people migrating (over fifty-five thousand per year into Houston during 1975 through 1983).

Sunbelt states are considered to be politically conservative, and their expanding influence is seen as an important element in the establishment of conservative values nationally.

Sunset Legislation

requires state legislators to periodically review government programs and agencies to assess their viability. This review, in effect, determines if the programs are still needed or should be allowed to "die," thus making the "sun set" for them.

The first "sunset law" was passed in Colorado in 1976. Sunset legislation again made news on December 31, 1984, when the Civil Aeronautics Board, a federal regulatory agency which no longer had anything to regulate, was dismantled under sunset provisions.

Proponents of the sunset-style review claim it forces lawmakers to periodically dismantle those agencies and programs which have outlived their usefulness. They see sunset legislation as a "partnership" between executive and legislative branches of government; a way of holding government accountable for the viability and usefulness of its programs. Opponents, on the other hand, see sunset laws as a way for lawmakers to strip away politically undesirable but still valuable services and programs.

Sunshine Legislation

is a law enacted by Congress in 1977 requiring all federal agencies to conduct their business in sessions open to the public. This law applies to all regulatory commissions, independent agencies, and advisory committees, but not to the major cabinet departments. The law also explicitly forbids "unofficial" meetings between government agency officials and people doing business with that agency.

The sunshine legislation is part of a general movement to remove secrecy from government wherever possible. It is a reaction to the Watergate disclosures of illegal and unethical conduct by public officials. The sunshine legislation encourages citizens to take legal action whenever an official meeting is closed to the public. Many states have adopted similar "open meeting" laws.

Superfund

is an Environmental Protection Agency (EPA) program to clean up the worst toxic waste dump sites in the United States.

According to the EPA, there are 378,000 toxic waste sites in the nation; 25,000 of these have been abandoned and 2,000 pose serious risks. The EPA has asked Congress to appropriate $11.7 billion for Superfund over the next five years. Congress is proposing $5.3 billion and has criticized the EPA for its tardiness in cleaning up 500 dump sites identified in 1983, and for grossly underestimating the cost of its cleanup programs.

The EPA contends that Superfund is hampered by a lack of standards outlining what degree of cleanup is needed to protect public health. Burial is the cheapest way to dispose of toxic wastes, but EPA officials say that burning, chemical treatment, and recycling are safer and more effective. In addition to disputes over methods and money, Superfund administrators seem unable to decide on which dumps to clean up first.

Synfuel

is short for synthetic fuel, and for the U.S. Synthetic Fuels Corporation, a government agency created to assist in the research and development of artificial alternatives to oil and gas.

Established in 1980 by the Carter Administration, the Synthetic Fuels Corporation was given a $19 billion budget for issuing loans and guarantees to aid private industry in developing effective gas and oil substitutes. The objective was to reduce U.S. dependence on foreign energy sources by devising new (and practical) ways to extract fuel from abundant materials such as coal and shale.

As of late 1984, the Synthetic Fuels Corporation had spent $3 billion on only a handful of projects. Critics charge that the agency is an inefficient bureaucracy spending too much on too little. To date, Synthetic Fuels has backed research that would produce fuel at double the cost of oil. The agency's goal was to produce the equivalent of half a million barrels of oil per day by 1987, and the equivalent of two million barrels per day by 1990. The three synfuel plants currently in operation can produce the equivalent of forty thousand barrels per day.

The synfuel approach has been hurt by the steady decline in the price of natural petroleum. For many potential synthetic fuel developers, the research doesn't seem worth it. Also lessening the need for synfuel is a 400-million barrel reserve of crude oil stored in Texas and Louisiana caverns. The reserve is seen as adequate protection against any disruption in U.S. foreign fuel sources.

Its supporters believe that the synfuel concept must be developed, and warn that oil imports are rising again after years of stability. But the world is suddenly rich in oil, so these warning have been, for the most part, unheeded.

Experts believe that Synthetic Fuels Corporation's budget will be cut drastically—at least by half. (*See* Coal Gassification)

Synthesizer

sound dominates "technopop" record hits, such as the Eurythmics' *Sweet Dreams are Made of This* and the soundtracks of the movies *Chariots of Fire, Scarface,* and *Gorky Park.*

Veteran songwriters and composers agree with young rockers that the synthesizer is the most provocative development in music today.

"A synthesizer works like a magnifying glass," says *Chariots of Fire* composer Vangelis. "With it you can go deeper into sound than you can with an acoustic instrument."

Synthesizers, which used to look like star-cruiser control *see*panels, are now smaller than Hammond organs. They generate tones electronically and approximate the sounds of conventional instruments so well that it's difficult for the untrained ear to tell the difference.

They can also produce a wide range of startling aural effects. "Synthesized sounds are as close as you can get to V-2 rockets, mortar blasts, and TV news," says a member of the rock group Devo.

Some musicians are becoming concerned that synthesizers may one day replace orchestras. Others doubt that will happen, claiming that synthesizer sound lacks the warmth and passion of "human" music.

Tax Reform

is any attempt to redesign the U.S. tax code. Also called "tax simplification," a tax-reform program usually involves reducing the number of tax brackets and doing away with many deductions and credits.

Tax-reform proposals are always opposed by special-interest groups that benefit from the existing structure. Most of the reform plans now circulating around Washington would cost corporations and some wealthy individuals their favorite write-offs.

The goal of tax reform is to raise revenue and spread the tax burden as fairly as possible across all levels of the taxpayer epopulation and the business community.

Some sort of modified flat tax is usually part of any tax-reform proposal. Some so-called tax reform plans are simply attempts by legislators to reduce their constituents' taxes at someone else's expense.

Tax Shelters

are investment programs specifically designed to take full advantage of accelerated depreciation schedules, investment tax credits, interest deductions, depletion allowances, and other (sometimes obscure) provisions of the U.S. tax code.

Shelters include investments in oil and natural-gas exploration ventures, office buildings, shopping centers, apartment complexes, factories, and industrial parks. Until the mid-1970s, tax shelters were used almost exclusively by the rich, but now they are marketed for the masses by firms which exist solely for the purpose of selling tax benefits.

In 1985, a report issued by Public Citizen (a public interest group organized by Ralph Nader) was highly critical of tax shelters: "The secret of tax shelters is that they produce artificial paper losses that aren't real losses but which still reduce taxes. The idea behind tax shelters is to invest one dollar for two or three dollars worth of deductions."

The higher the income of the investor, the more beneficial a tax shelter becomes. Tax shelter offerings totaled an estimated $49 billion in 1984, at least 25 percent of which was diverted to promoters, packagers, lawyers, and accountants. In addition to the tax revenue lost to shelters (about $20 billion annually), they absorbed a great deal of investment capital which might have gone for expanded or new businesses, new products, and new jobs.

All tax shelters, of course, are not without merit. Many were enacted to encourage development and growth. Municipal bonds, trust funds for children's education, IRAs, and investments in energy conservation or urban construction are considered beneficial to the nation's interest and the interests of its citizens.

Technocrat

is a scientist or engineer who directly or indirectly exerts political power or makes policy. Recently, the term has been applied to artificial transplant advocates and space militarists. In the past it has been used to describe Soviet leaders or anyone who advocates "rule by technology."

Teenage Suicide

has more than doubled over the past thirty years. The five thousand teenagers who take their own lives each year make suicide the second leading cause of death (behind auto accidents) among young people.

Concerned child psychologists called teenage suicide "a national tragedy of enormous proportions." Its causes are family instability, alienation, severe depression, and alcohol and drug abuse. Teenage suicide often occurs in tragic clusters—three in Wyoming in the spring of 1984, six in a Texas community a few months later.

After the airing of a television movie purporting to examine the problem of teenage suicide, and publication of a *People* magazine story on the same subject, psychologists and social workers criticized the media for exploiting the issue, turning a tragedy into a fad. One psychologist called the television movie's suicide scene, in which a young couple killed themselves with carbon monoxide fumes, "a training film." Several "copycat" suicides occurred during the week after the film was shown.

Experts see teenage suicide as a cry for attention, or the ultimate revenge. Obviously, experts say, kids don't really understand the finality of death. A teenage suicide causes severe trauma for the victim's family and friends, many of whom blame themselves for the death.

Suicidal symptoms include drastic changes in behavior, almost complete withdrawal from friends, a lack of interest in normal activities, jokes about death, and the giving away of possessions.

(CIA) Terror Manual,

explaining the techniques of political assassination and guerrilla warfare, was discovered in the possession of Nicaraguan contras (*see* Nicaragua) in October 1984.

The manual advocates the hiring of "professional criminals" to carry out selective acts of terrorism (assassinations, bombings) and suggests that the rebels kill sympathizers from time to time, "to create martyrs."

A comic book version of the manual taught less violent techniques which civilians could use to subvert "the traitorous Marxist state": the stuffing of toilets with paper, making bogus reservations at hotels, and disrupting mail delivery and traffic.

The manual was apparently based on a lesson plan used to train Special Forces troops in Vietnam. Its discovery brought angry responses from Congress, embarrassed the Reagan administration, and led to an investigation of improper conduct within the CIA.

Opinion on the manual was mixed: CIA officials dismissed it as the product of a lower-level staff member's "inadvisable zeal." The Nicaraguan government took the manual more seriously, calling it "proof of the U.S. official policy of state terrorism."

Third World

refers to a large bloc of nations characterized by underdeveloped economies, overdependence on agriculture or mineral extraction, low per capita and national income, unstable or dictatorial political systems, rampant population growth, hunger, and poor health care. Most recently, much of the Third World has been characterized by an increasing hostility to the developed nations in general and the United States in particular.

The term "Third World" originated during the Cold War of the 1950s. It expressed a growing feeling among students of geopolitics that while the most powerful nations of the world had polarized into two "worlds"—the capitalist Western democracies and the Eastern European Communist states—a "Third World" of powerless, economically underdeveloped nations had been left on the sidelines.

More than one hundred nations are still considered Third World. Together they wield substantial influence in the U.N. General Assembly, but it is a serious mistake to consider the Third World a monolithic bloc.

Some Third World nations (Ethiopia, Angola, and South Yemen, for example) are securely in the Communist camp. Others, such as Egypt, Pakistan, and Indonesia are friendly to the United States. While most Third World nations remain poor, oil brought enormous, though narrowly distributed, wealth to countries such as Saudi Arabia. Other Third World nations have emerged as independent powers. China recently has experienced a surge in economic progress and India, while still poor by Western standards, has begun growing enough food to feed its people and has established a government which successfully manages a large, complex, and ethnically diverse society.

Three-Martini Lunch

is a phrase used to refer to the wide array of loopholes and questionable deductions enjoyed by businesspeople. The phrase was used by Jimmy Carter to gain working-class support for business-tax reform. Because many business executives now drink Perrier and white wine at lunch, the term is probably outdated, although the sentiment it symbolized is not. Several 1985 tax reform plans targeted business deductions for elimination.

Toxic Shock Syndrome (TSS),

a serious consequence of staph bacterial infections, causes failure of bodily functions (shock), often resulting in coma, and sometimes death. A curious effect of toxic shock syndrome is the loss of skin from the palms of the hands and the soles of the feet.

Most of the public believes that toxic shock syndrome was eradicated in 1980 when Rely tampons were taken off the market, but this is not the case.

The first case of toxic shock syndrome was identified in 1977 by Dr. James K. Todd. By 1979, dozens of toxic shock syndrome cases had been reported. Although the Centers for Disease Control in Atlanta (CDC) found a connection between the disease and tampons, specifically with the Rely brand tampon, they never claimed tampons were the cause of the disease.

This important distinction was not adequately highlighted immediately by the media, and the toxic shock tampon link dominated the news for about six months in 1980. Dr. Todd called the publicity "alarmist nonsense—the toxic *schlock* syndrome." People began calling Todd "Dr. Tampon" and offering peculiar theories about the source of the disease.

In 1983, researchers announced that the bacterial gene apparently responsible for the toxin in TSS had been identified. An important benefit of this discovery will possibly be the ability to administer simple blood tests to women of childbearing age, the highest risk TSS group. Fortunately, most women have antibodies which protect them from developing TSS.

Triathlon,

an athletic event popularized by the so-called Iron Man competition, is an endurance race combining a twenty-five-mile run, a one hundred-mile bicycle race, and a five-mile swim. The event requires vast reservoirs of strength and endurance.

In 1985, Dr. Steven Jonas, a professor of Preventative Medicine at the University of New York Medical School, introduced a version of the triathlon in which normal humans could compete. Jonas calls his event the mini-triathlon. It consists of a ten-mile run, a fifteen-mile bicycle race, and a one and one-half-mile swim.

"Virtually anyone in reasonable physical and mental shape can do a mini-triathlon without turning their lives upside down," Jonas said. "The major requirements are consistency and regularity." Jonas claims to have designed a training schedule which will allow almost anyone to complete a mini-triathlon after workouts of five hours per week for thirteen weeks.

According to Jonas, triathloning has a number of attractive benefits, including cardiovascular fitness (which reduces the risk of heart disease). Additionally, Jonas said, "Training makes you feel good. It sets you up for the day. It gets your blood going, cleans your mind, and gives you energy. And, it has a calming effect."

Jonas has run marathons (twenty-six miles, three hundred yards) and believes that the triathlon is easier on the body because of the opportunities to coast during the bicycle race and to float during the swimming segment. The doctor has written a book on triathloning "for ordinary mortals" which will be published in 1985.

Trident

is a submarine-launched ballistic missile (SLBM) developed by the U.S. Navy. The missile, which is thirty-four feet long and weighs thirty-two tons, has a range of six thousand miles. Its navigation system follows the stars to find its target. The Trident carries eight powerful nuclear warheads in a MIRV (see MIRV) configuration. From sixteen to twenty-four Trident missiles are carried on each U.S. nuclear submarine.

Trivial Pursuit (Research)

is based on the best-selling board game of the 1980s that tests players' knowledge of (sometimes obscure) facts in such areas as history, entertainment, sports, popular culture, the arts, and science. There are now many specialized versions of the game, including a popular one entitled "Baby Boomer," designed to capitalize on the post-war baby-boom generation.

Late in 1984, researchers at New Jersey's Fairleigh Dickinson University conducted experiments in memory recall. Using Trivial Pursuit questions, participants were asked to "think out loud" in their attempt to retrieve items from memory.

The researchers concluded that people employ a variety of memory techniques, including visualization, logic, and free association to recall such diverse items as celebrity names and the color of the first and last stripes of the American flag.

John Keselica, a professor of experimental psychology and administrator of the Trivial Pursuit research, believes that the game is popular because "it keeps us in touch with our personal history."

Truth Seekers,

a non-profit group, aids adoptees and natural parents trying to find each other. For a $50 membership fee, Truth Seekers assigns a research assistant to people trying to track down their natural families. The group also holds monthly meetings to lend support to those going through an emotionally draining process.

The growth in the number of adoptees and "birth mothers" looking for each other has spawned a thriving, mostly underground industry of tracers, state and nationwide registries, and even a national magazine called *People Finders* (which runs more than three thousand personal ads each month).

In most cases, adoption files are sealed and can be opened only through a court order. This secrecy has created an "information black market" in which adoptees and mothers are constantly being victimized by unqualified researchers—or "fixers"—who use theft and bribery to secure court and hospital records.

Truth Seekers helps its members avoid the pitfalls of the black market. The organization advocates the opening of adoption files to eliminate the underground ripoffs, but opponents of the plan contend that open files could very well lead to kidnapping by natural parents, marital difficulties when a "secret" child turns up, and compel many women to choose abortion over adoption.

Currently, two states in the United States have an open-records policy. Six others allow "search and consent" procedures, in which the parent or child being sought must consent before adoption information is released.

Type A Behavior,

according to Dr. Ray Rosenman and R. Meyer Friedman, the San Francisco cardiologists who coined the term, is a dangerous living pattern characterized by a compelling sense of urgency.

The doctors call Type A behavior "hurry sickness" and contend that the lifestyle associated with it is a major cause of heart attacks. Type A people refuse to relax. They are relentlessly aggressive, highly competitive, and unnecessarily hostile. They eat too much, worry about things they can't control, talk too fast, and frequently interrupt others. Type A behavior is common among successful executives.

Type B behavior, Rosenman and Friedman suggest, considerably reduces the risk of heart attack. Type B people keep their work and other elements of their lives in perspective. They adopt a calm, balanced outlook, relax and exercise frequently, enjoy themselves, their families and friends, eat cautiously, and do not allow outside pressures to overwhelm them.

Ultimate Microscope,

or the electron microscope, which is being built at the University of Chicago, will be five times more powerful than any existing microscope, and will enable scientists to see between atoms and learn how atoms interact and behave in small groups.

Many of the microscope's parts require precision tooling, with margins of error of less than fifty-millionths of an inch. Components should be completed by the end of 1985, but Professor Albert Crewe, the inventor of the electron microscope who is supervising its construction, is unsure about when the device will become operational.

"I hope to have everything bolted together by the end of this year," Crewe said. "But then you have several hundred knobs to twiddle. It might take us some time to do all the twiddling and get everything to work. It could be weeks, months, or even years."

Unemployment Statistics,

compiled by the government, are estimates of the number of unemployed in the United States.

Directors of state and county welfare departments, executives of government sponsored job-training programs, and labor union leaders all contend that the official unemployment figures are seriously understated.

The process through which unemployment statistics are compiled consists of forty-three steps, beginning with a household survey.

Counted among the employed is anyone who is paid for at least one hour of work during the week that includes the twelfth day of the month.

Unemployment totals count only those who are actively seeking work. Not included are discouraged workers who have given up trying to find a job, or part-time workers looking for full-time employment.

The Bureau of Labor Statistics, which is responsible for compiling unemployment estimates, adjusts national totals by applying historical unemployment data for the self employed, family workers, and agricultural workers.

United Nations Educational Scientific and Cultural Organization (UNESCO)

was established to promote understanding and cooperation among nations. The U.N. agency promotes technological and cultural exchanges, and works with other U.N. agencies to assist developing countries in growth and modernization programs.

Among UNESCO's goals are the improvement of education at all levels, the expansion of cooperative scientific research (especially in the areas of energy and environmental protection), and the preservation of national monuments and treasures.

UNESCO has more than 140 member nations, but the United States is no longer among them. Early in 1985, the United States withdrew from UNESCO charging that the organization had become wasteful and corrupt under a director and staff who had squandered hundreds of million of dollars— much of which was contributed by American taxpayers.

Columnist William Safire applauded the U.S. withdrawal, calling UNESCO a "playpen for Third World diplomats." (See Third World) Safire also charged that UNESCO was "blatantly antifreedom, anti-United States, and anti-Israel."

Urban Enterprise Zones

are designated areas in which new businesses can receive tax breaks and other incentives from local and state governments.

There are 1,130 enterprise zones in nineteen states. Most are in depressed city areas with high unemployment levels. The zones were established in anticipation of federal legislation President Reagan advocated strongly in 1982, and again in his 1985 State of the Union address. The federal enterprise-zone bill has twice passed the Senate but has run into trouble in the House of Representatives.

According to Rep. Joseph McDade (R-Pa), "These zones change areas that are revenue draining into areas where there are people going off welfare and onto payrolls. They pay taxes, and the new buildings and companies add to the local and state revenue base. There's surely some lag time between the loss due to the incentives and the addition to the tax revenues due to investments and jobs, but it would never be more than two years in the most extreme case."

Rep. Dan Rostenkowski (D-Il), chairman of the House Ways and Means Committee, was unimpressed by the enterprise-zone concept. "One obvious problem is that it loses revenue at a time we're trying to reduce a huge deficit. The zones are an open-ended drain on revenues," Rostenkowski said.

The Treasury Department has established that a federal enterprise-zone program would cost the government $3.4 billion in its first five years. There has been no official government study on the gains in jobs and investments in the enterprise zones already established by state and local governments, but a 1983 report by the Sabre Foundation, a public policy group, indicated that nine states that created 180 enterprise zones attracted about $500 million in investments and twenty thousand new jobs.

Waffling

is to talk indecisively or elusively. Politicians waffle frequently. The term comes from the Scottish *waff* which means to flutter like a clumsy bird and never land anywhere.

War Powers Act,

enacted in 1973, is intended to ensure that the president will rely on the collective judgment of Congress when authorizing the use of U.S. armed forces in "hostilities."

According to the Constitution, only Congress is empowered to declare wars and provide military forces to fight them. Even so, before the War Powers Act was passed, American troops had been sent into military engagements 199 times without a congressional declaration of war. Largely a reaction to the Vietnam war, the War Powers Act attempts to reaffirm congressional authority in decisions involving American troops.

Under the act, the president can commit armed forces only after declaration of war by Congress; by specific congressional authority; or when an attack on U.S. forces creates a national emergency. In a national emergency, the president must withdraw U.S. troops within "sixty to ninety days" unless war is declared.

Congress compromised on the act's provisions in the Lebanon (*see* Lebanon) crisis, and President Reagan avoided consulting the legislature in the Grenada (*see* Grenada) invasion by withdrawing U.S. troops within the ninety-day limit.

Warsaw Pact

is a military alliance of the USSR and its Eastern European satellites. The Soviets consider the alliance a counterforce to NATO, the North Atlantic Treaty Organization of Western nations (*see* NATO), and use it to maintain control of its Eastern European satellites.

The Warsaw Treaty was signed in 1955, one week after a rearmed West Germany joined NATO. Warsaw Pact members include the Soviet Union, Romania, Bulgaria, Czechoslovakia, East Germany, Hungary, and Poland. Alliance troops operate as one unified army under Soviet command. Hungary (in 1956), Poland and Czechoslovakia (in 1968) have attempted to withdraw from the Warsaw Pact group, but were dragged back into the alliance through military force.

Warsaw Pact nations have a huge edge in conventional (non-nuclear) weapons and troop concentrations over NATO.

Wellness,

according to a growing legion of advocates, is more than the absence of disease, it is a mode of living structured to *prevent* illness and minimize deterioration. Too many people, wellness adherents point out, take better care of their cars than their bodies.

Diet, fitness, and the avoidance of negative stress are the major components of a wellness program. Advocates eat little or no red meat and avoid salt, fats, sugars, and caffeine. A wellness-oriented diet is built around fish, poultry, fruits, and vegetables. Regular exercise complements the diet. Vacations are spent hiking in the mountains or "recharging" vital bodily systems at health spas. Wellness advocates view smoking and excessive alcohol consumption as deadly abuses to be avoided at all costs.

Like any philosophy, wellness has its fanatics—people who become obsessed with their bodies to such an extent that other aspects of life are ignored. For the most part, however, wellness regimens are sensible, nurturing an increased vitality that improves the quality of life.

A growing number of U.S. physicians reject the notion that the bulk of this nation's health-care resources should continue to be directed toward the development of expensive high-technology treatment techniques (the artificial heart, for instance). Greater emphasis on preventative medicine is needed, these experts say. Several legislators agree and have attempted to establish wellness-oriented programs under government sponsorship, contending that greater attention to preventative measures now would substantially reduce the costs of Medicare and similar programs later.

Whip

is an assistant floor leader. In Congress and in state legislatures each party has a whip, who acts much like a foreman on a cattle ranch, rounding up party legislators when there's voting to be done.

The duties of a party whip include canvassing fellow party members on key issues and counting their votes; marshalling full party voting strength on all issues the party considers critical; and acting as party chief when the floor leader is absent.

Whips are selected in party caucuses (see Caucus), usually on the recommendation of party leaders.

Winter Depression

is a mood decline which occurs during the winter months. Victims of winter depression slow down noticeably, frequently oversleep, and crave carbohydrates. In spring and summer, these same people are elated, active, energetic, and generally function well.

Researchers have noted that people who suffer from winter depression experience seasonal rhythms of activity, appetite, and sleep similar to other mammals (bears being the most obvious example).

In 1985, scientists at the National Institute of Mental Health found that day length was an important variable which might be manipulated to control winter depression. The institute exposed a group of winter-depression sufferers to increased light—equal to the brightness of clear spring sunshine —from early morning until about 8:00 P.M.

The researchers observed marked improvement in mood, and noted that depression returned when the artificial sunlight was withheld. They also noticed that the intensity of light seemed to be critical to the mood improvement—standard indoor illumination was ineffective.

Scientists are not able to explain why bright light alleviates winter depression, but reports suggest that the light may suppress the secretion of a hormone called melatonin.

One of many hormones implicated in depression, melatonin is usually secreted at night.

World Bank,

a United Nations agency established in 1944 to assist European recovery after World War II, is officially called the International Bank for Reconstruction and Development (IBRD). It has become the most important lending agency in international development, distributing funds from wealthy nations to poor countries in an attempt to improve the world economy.

Nearly all the non-Communist nations of the world are members of the World Bank. The wealthier nations, especially the United States, control loans; voting on loan decisions is weighted according to a member nation's contribution to World Bank assets.

In the early 1950s, the agency's focus shifted from reconstruction in war-torn countries to loans and technical assistance in underdeveloped areas. Projects currently funded by the World Bank include dams, irrigation systems, railroads, mining operations, and factory construction.

The World Bank made news in 1984 when officials in the Reagan administration criticized the agency for lending Third World nations money to pay foreign debts.

World Court,

officially the International Court of Justice, is a United Nations agency headquartered at The Hague in the Netherlands.

The court, which consists of fifteen judges each from a different country, was established to settle international disputes. No nation is required to bring disputes before the World Court, but nations that subscribe to its charter are obliged to abide by the courts rulings.

In April 1984, Nicaragua filed charges with the World Court claiming that the United States, through the mining of Nicaraguan harbors and other activities, was engaged in a concentrated attempt to overthrow the Sandinista government.

In January 1985, the State Department announced that the United States would not participate in Nicaragua's suit. The United States charged that the World Court had no jurisdiction in the matter and that Nicaragua's case was a "misuse of the court for political purposes." U.S. officials walked out of the court and stated that the United States would not abide by any World Court decision related to Central America for two years.

Nicaragua condemned the U.S. walkout calling it "a clear negation of the most elementary principles that govern relations among nations." In the United States, several lawyers and Democratic Congressmen worried about the effect that the U.S. decision would have on the nation's international reputation and on the future of the World Court.

World Health Organization

is a U.N. agency that works to improve the health of people throughout the world—especially in Third World nations (see Third World). Its efforts have helped to check the proliferation of many serious diseases. The World Health Organization distributes vaccines and medical equipment, presents health education programs, and assists developing countries in contraception and sanitation efforts.

Zinc Gluconate,

a mineral compound sold over-the-counter as a nutritional supplement, has been found to reduce the duration of the common cold.

A report published in 1984 by David R. Davis, a University of Texas researcher, indicated that 90 percent of participating cold sufferers who took zinc gluconate tablets lost all cold symptoms within seven days. About a third of the group recovered from their colds within twenty-four hours.

The researchers who conducted the zinc study reported only minor side effects—an objectionable taste and mouth irritation.

INDEX